GEORGE MACDONALD

GEORGE MACDONALD
A Short Life

ELIZABETH SAINTSBURY

CANONGATE

First published in Great Britain in 1987
by Canongate Publishing Ltd. 17 Jeffrey Street Edinburgh

Typeset by Chatsworth Publicity Services Newcastle upon Tyne

Printed and bound in Great Britain by
Billings & Sons

British Library Cataloguing in Publication Data

Saintsbury, Elizabeth
George MacDonald
MacDonald, George, *1824-1905* — Biography
Authors, Scottish — 19th century — Biography
I. Title
823'.8   PR4968

ISBN 0-86241—092—4

CONTENTS

ACKNOWLEDGEMENTS

My grateful thanks are due to Mr. Norman G. Connell,
Mrs. M. Black of Greenkirtle, Huntly and the Librarian
of the Brander Library, Huntly for their help and
advice; to Mrs. Freda Levson a descendant of George
MacDonald and a founder member of the Society which
bears his name, for some unique family photographs;
to staff at the National Library of Scotland, for
assistance with research; and to David Robb at Dundee
University for his corrections and suggestions.
My thanks also to the Hammersmith Central Library for the use

Romantic Heritage

George MacDonald was fiercely proud of his highland heritage. He loved the outward symbols of the Celtic way of life: the music of bagpipes and harp, and the wearing of tartan and claymore. For these were expressions of love for his native land, independence of spirit and reverence for the heroic deeds of his forebears. The MacDonalds and the MacIans (a particular tribe belonging to the Clan) were renowned for their poetic powers and in the Highlanders' poetry was enshrined the wisdom of their race.

MacDonald's forebears belonged to Clan Ranald. Young Clan Ranald, the son of the chief, was one of the first to join Charles Edward Stuart when he landed on the west coast of Scotland in 1745 to prove by force his right of succession to the throne. It was on the chief's territory that the Prince landed and Clan Ranald sent seven hundred men to join the Young Pretender's army. In 1715 at the time of the Jacobite rising in support of the Old Pretender, most of the clans were still Catholic and in sympathy with his cause, but by 1745 Presbyterianism established by the Protestant William and Mary in 1690 was more firmly entrenched in Scotland and there was less whole-hearted support from the Chieftans for the Jacobite cause. Also the memory of the punishment and exile suffered by the last rebels must have been some deterrent to those chieftans who had begun to enjoy a period of relative peace.

Among those who did rally to the cause was a contingent from Portsoy on the north Banffshire coast. Here was a settlement of a few families living above the rocky shore where a beautiful pink and white marble was quarried as it still is today. The local register, compiled to record the names of those who joined the Jacobite forces, lists one William MacDonald, the official piper, a resident of Portsoy, the great grandfather of George MacDonald. William's father had migrated to the district with his father when they escaped from Glencoe and they earned a living by quarrying and polishing marble. William and his family spoke Gaelic and were Catholic, so instead of following Sir William Dunbar like most Portsoy volunteers, he marched with the Catholic Frasers. William and his son were inevitably involved in the general defeat of the Jacobites at Culloden in 1746. Tragically William had been blinded in the battle but guided by his eldest son fled from the field and embarked on a hazardous flight along the Morayshire coast in the direction of his home at Portsoy.

But retribution at the hands of the militia would be awaiting any rebels who had survived the campaign. The Jacobites' supporters therefore did not dare to return home but found temporary refuge in caves along the Banffshire coast not far from Portsoy. Here their friends and supporters fed them. The fugitives' ordeal is fictitiously but graphically described by George MacDonald in his novel *Malcolm*. In this book the town of Portlossie corresponds in layout to that of Cullen, a town in the area which he knew well.

> The seatown of Portlossie was as irregular a gathering of small cottages as could be found on the surface of the globe. They faced every way, turning their backs and gables every way — only of the roofs could you predict the position — they were divided from each other by every sort of small irregular space and passage and looked like a national assembly debating a constitution. Close behind the 'seaton' as it was called, ran a highway climbing far above the chimneys of the village to the level of the town above. Behind this road and separated from it by a high wall of stone, lay a succession of heights and hollows covered with grass. In front of the cottage lay sand and sea.

It is impossible to identify the exact cave where William and his son took refuge as there are many in the area, and the rocky coastline is constantly changing with the battering of frequent storms. But in *Malcolm* the main character penetrates into the recesses of a cave called 'Bailies Barn' and discovers another one concealed behind. The novel fictionalizes events that had actually occurred generations before in the MacDonald family. When Malcolm finds this secret chamber, 'he knew he had come upon a cave in which his great grandfather had found refuge so many years ago.'

William MacDonald and his son survived in such a cave for six months in hunger, cold and constant danger of discovery. Later in the same year, 1746, Parliament passed a Disarming Act prohibiting the wearing of clan tartans, condemning the pipes, and abolishing the hereditary jurisdiction of chiefs over the members of their clans.

Eventually, however, William and his son were able to return home, but his wife had died of shock on the day the defeat at Culloden was announced.

The MacDonalds had had a small farm at Portsoy but it was confiscated in the aftermath of Culloden. Robert Falconer's grandmother, in the novel *Robert Falconer*, describes it to him as 'a wheen houses and a kailyard or two wi' a bit fairmy on the top of a cauld hill near the seashore.'

The Little Grey Town

The youngest of William MacDonald's children, Charles Edward, named after the Young Pretender, was educated at Fordyce Academy, only a mile or two inland from Portsoy. This school had a good scholastic record and was well known even before a certain Bombay businessman named Smith, a native of Fordyce, endowed it with his name. Charles Edward was intelligent and hard-working with a good business sense. At first he was apprenticed to a weaving business. This gave him an introduction to the trade and also the opportunity for advancement. He was offered a clerkship in the bleaching business of McVeagh Brothers at Huntly in Aberdeenshire.

Huntly, described by George MacDonald as 'The Little Grey Town,' is situated on a triangular piece of land between the rivers Bogie and Deveron. In *Robert Falconer* the town is called Rothieden and in *Alec Forbes*, Glamerton, but in both cases it bears a strong resemblance to the writer's own beloved Huntly.

Huntly is girdled about with low hills — a soft green in summer and heather-clad in autumn, shadowed here and there with clumps of pine, their rounded contours broken by the thrust of Clashmach and beyond the Tap o' Noth crowned with its vitrified fort. This is as George MacDonald saw it through the eyes of Robert Falconer from his grandmother's house on the corner of Church Street: 'one blue truncated peak in the distance.'

The town's growth and prosperity such as it was when Charles Edward MacDonald moved there in the 1770s, depended on its proximity to the River Bogie whose waters contained chemical properties necessary for the bleaching of linen and other materials made from flax.

The Bogie rises in the west, over two thousand feet up near the Buck of Cabrach, once, as the name suggests, the haunt of deer. At first the Bogie is the merest trickle but as it joins forces with the many rain-swelled streams tumbling down the hillside, it flows more swiftly and becomes the Water of Bogie, passing through a ravine close to Craig Castle at the base of a mountain, the Tap o' Noth and eventually, after skirting the east side of the town falls into the wider and swifter Deveron river to the north of Huntly beyond the castle. The golden Deveron journeys through a different terrain, rising also near the remote fastness of Cabrach but making its way through forest land bordering Haugh of Glass and bearing its peaty waters over rocks and boulders to join the Bogie. When the river is swollen with torrential rain, it can be terrifying. Serious floods can occur such as George MacDonald describes in *Alec Forbes* probably from first-hand memory of the flood in 1829 when he was only five years old.

> 'With what a roar the Wan Water (Deveron) came down its rocks, rushing from its steeper course into the slow incline of the Glamour (Bogie). A terrible country they came from — those two ocean-bound rivers up among the hilltops. There on the desolate peat-moss spongy black and cold, the rain was pouring into the awful holes whence generations had dug their fuel and into the natural chasms of the earth, soaking the soil and sending torrents, like the flaxen hair of a Titanic Naiad rolling into the bosom of the rising River — God below ..... By and by the pools would be filled and the hidden caves ... their sides would give way, the waters would rush from one into the other and from all down the hillsides the sponge would be drained off.'

In this flood the bridge over the Bogie was washed away and several people drowned. In *Alec Forbes*, the wooden bridge was washed away, drowning the schoolmaster and the crippled pupil he was trying to rescue. But in the winter the river was held in the binding power of the frost and its frozen waters chilled and stiffened to ice. Then it became a children's playground.

Long before the development of the bleaching business the town owed its existence to Huntly Castle, from Norman times the home of the Gordons. Traders and labourers settled near the Castle and in what was known until the end of the eighteenth century as the Raws of Strathbogie. Although now an uninhabited ruin, the castle has still the romantic air of a medieval palace and retains some of its early features — the Norman Motte, for example, high above the rocky bed of the Deveron river, and the thick walls of the medieval keep known as Auld Werk. At the close of the sixteenth century the first Marquis of Huntly converted the old castle into a Renaissance palace, building a stately pile with lofty oriel windows, stone-mullioned but glassless now, grand doorways on which were carved armorial bearings or quaint heraldic devices. Inside were splendid fireplaces with ornamental carvings. Huntly Castle though roofless is a fairly extensive building with the staircases well preserved especially the spiral stairs in the turreted tower and those leading down to the dank cellars and dungeon-like rooms below ground. The castle retains a somewhat eerie atmosphere. Although it has been uninhabited since the Gordon family left it in 1752, it is still an important feature of the town. It is maintained by the Ministry of the Environment and attracts hundreds of visitors each year. Even in the MacDonalds' time it was a place to visit. In *Alec Forbes,* Alec makes a point of taking his cousin Kate there one evening when she was staying with his family and frightened her nearly out of her wits with the creaking floors, falling masonry and the dust of ages which covered everything.

The Gordons moved to Fochabers, but on the death of the third Duke his widow moved back to Huntly and rebuilt nearby Huntly Lodge using some of the stones from the Castle. It is now a hotel and lies about a quarter of a mile away over the bridge which spans the Deveron. But the influence of the Gordon family did not come to an end. The last Duchess left her mark on the town for posterity by building in 1841 the splendid school which bears her name, and to this day provides an education for all the children of Huntly and the surrounding countryside.

Gradually the inhabitants of the Raws of Strathbogie whose source of livelihood had moved northwards, extended the village southwards. Then cottages were mainly of stone with thatched roofs and many of them had a second floor which housed looms. The chief occupation for women was weaving. The town developed symmetrically along two straight streets which intersected each other in an open square. Here the population gathered. The women frequented the market stalls. Those from outlying farms came with baskets of produce: butter, cheese, eggs and poultry which the townswomen were eager to bargain for. The men gathered in the thatched and gabled Inn, predecessor of the Gordon Arms, to discuss their crops, the price of fatstock and of course the weather, over a pint of ale. It was a Crofters' world. Their talk was all in Gaelic. George MacDonald as a boy recalls rushing out of school on a market day and slipping into the Gordon Arms to listen to the conversation. He never learnt the Gaelic himself and had a struggle to make out what the crofters were saying. But all the same he absorbed a surprising amount of information about life on a farm.

Stalls were erected round the wall in the centre of the Square where now stands the statue of Charles Lennox Gordon, 5th Duke of Richmond a benefactor to industry in Huntly. In addition to farm produce all kinds of commodities were sold: sweets, ribbons, laces and neckerchiefs as well as strips of resinous bog-fir for candles to give light in the cotters' dwellings. These were brought into the town in carts drawn by rough-coated horses, together with bags of cranberries in their season, and juniper berries to be used in flavouring beer. When Charles Edward MacDonald came to Huntly in the 1770s, the goods being marketed would have provided some colour in an otherwise sombre scene, as the women wore duffle grey with white mutches, and the men, forbidden their colourful kilts and plaids, dun coloured knee-breeches and tailed coats of home-spun cloth.

Twice a day the square would be enlivened by the arrival of the mail coach, the crack of the post-horn warning of its approach. It was a splendid splash of scarlet, sometimes encrusted with sparkling snow, and drawn by four horses. At the hostelry these would be exchanged for fresh ones and the mail, the passengers and their luggage disgorged while bystanders stood around curiously like Robert Falconer pensively watching the arrival of Mary St John. The mail coach travelled between Aberdeen and the west.

The factory where Charles Edward went to work was situated in what is now called McVeagh Street. Charles Edward proved himself a good businessman and soon obtained a partnership in the firm and eventually became the owner. He extended the scope of the business by building a linen thread spinning factory in nearby MacDonald Street. Most of the population of Huntly was involved in the spinning and bleaching industry in a smaller or lesser way. Linen manufacture was booming although it was soon to be threatened by the import of cotton. In Charles Edward's factory the looms were driven by hand on the same principle as that employed in Hargreaves' spinning jenny patented in 1764. But its modification by Arkwright for the use of horse or water power probably led to its becoming uneconomic. As early as 1789 the first steam driven cotton factory had been established in Manchester. In George MacDonald's time the factory had been closed for a number of years, deserted though not pulled down. George must have frequented it as a boy and been intrigued by its ghostly appearance with the looms standing idle and silent and a thick film of dust on everything. It was here that Robert Falconer went secretly to play the forbidden and stolen violin, forcing his way through the overgrown garden with neglected gooseberry and currant bushes, into the stone and timber building now showing signs of decay. He found the rusting machinery 'with thread still in the spools and oil dried in the sockets'. He could almost see in imagination 'a woman seated at each of those silent powers set the whole frame in motion with its numberless spindles and spools rapidly revolving − a vague mystery of endless threads in orderly complication ... so that the whole place was full of a tumult of work, every little reel contributing its share'.

Charles Edward gave up the linen spinning but he retained the bleaching business even though trade was beginning to fall off on account of an alternative method having been discovered by his wife's cousin Charles Macintosh, using chloride of lime. Now he bleached cotton as well as linen. He had married in 1778 Isabella Robertson the daughter of a linen weaver. She was a remarkable woman ten years younger than himself, although at the time of their marriage illiterate, as her father would not allow her to learn to read or write. They had nine children, four boys and five girls, four of whom died in infancy.

In Robert Falconer's grandmother can be found a vivid portrait of Isabella MacDonald: stern, bigoted, uncompromising and upright yet with deep affections which she kept hidden as though she were almost afraid of showing them even to herself. 'Her conscience was more tender than her feelings .... The first relation she bore to most who came near her was one of severity and rebuke but underneath her cold outside lay a warm heart to which conscience acted the part of a somewhat capricious stoker, now quenching its heat with the cold water of duty, now stirring it up with the poker of reproach .... In doing the kindest thing in the world she would speak in a tone of command even of rebuke .... Frivolity was in her eyes a vice and this included violin playing'. Isabella MacDonald was also a rabid teetotaller even stipulating that no alcohol was to be drunk at her funeral.

Charles Edward did not confine himself to the bleaching business. He became a bank agent and looked after people's valuables on the same premises in which the bleaching was carried on. His wife took this side of the business seriously and organized the family Chanter Kist, a carved oak chest in which family records and heirlooms were usually kept, as a form of safe.

By this time the MacDonalds had ceased to be Catholics. Charles Edward was an elder in the Parish (Presbyterian) Church. But the established Church was then spiritually at a low ebb. The ministers were subject to patronage and were often more interested in hanging on to their social position than in preaching the gospel. George Cowie had founded a Secession Church in 1760 as a protest against the Establishment and had many supporters. Its denomination was congregational and its aim evangelisation of ordinary people. Its supporters were called missionars. It was to this church that Isabella MacDonald took her children. The preaching was uncompromisingly calvinistic with an emphasis on hell fire and predestination. Although at the close of the eighteenth century George Cowie was driven out of his pulpit by a decree of the General Assembly, he returned a few years later and built a new independent chapel in McVeagh Street. It is still standing today but with the union of the congregationalists with the free churches in Scotland in 1970 it became redundant and is now the Strathbogie Bakery. A relic of its original use is to be found preserved in the museum at the Brander Library in Huntly Square – a stained glass window taken from the church giving the information that George MacDonald preached there.

George Cowie was succeeded as minister by John Hill who was a great personal friend of the MacDonald's second son George who became a deacon and father of the novelist. The eldest, William, started a brewery in a disused bleach-works. Being twelve years older than George he was more independent of his brothers. Next came George and then Charles and James. The three younger boys all entered the family business, Charles being responsible for the banking. Unfortunately he turned out to be too easy-going, good-natured and anxious to please his customers and by injudicious money-lending soon got himself and the bank into debt, much to the grief of his mother, who while deploring the financial tangle in which the family was placed, feared more for the safety of her son's immortal soul. To escape imprisonment Charles fled to America leaving the family struggling to pay off the debt well into the next generation.

Isabella's agonizing is well depicted in Mrs Falconer's secret mourning for her son Andrew, Robert's father. The interview which took place between Grannie Falconer and her son is based on an occasion in 1835 which George MacDonald the writer, then only a boy of eleven, himself recalls. He remembered a stranger calling at the house who was really his Uncle Charles. The two were closeted together in a room in his grandmother's house for a long time. The other two brothers George and James now the sole partners in the bleaching business were responsible for discharging the debt. George recounted the episode to his son Greville who mentioned it in the biography of his parents.

For some time bleaching had become less profitable and the MacDonalds needed another source of income. In 1821 they obtained from the Duke of Gordon a lease of land at Upper

11

Pirriesmill. The property was situated to the east of the town beyond the bridge and bordering the river Bogie. It was waste land and difficult to farm but the brothers worked hard and soon got it into a state of sufficient cultivation to produce grass for a bleaching field and pasture for cattle.

This was the year too in which George MacDonald married Helen MacKay, a beautiful and well-educated woman. Her brother was a Gaelic scholar and friend of Sir Walter Scott. She proved a devoted wife and mother but their married life was prematurely ended when she died of tuberculosis ten years later. From the outset of the marriage Helen had been delicate and she was unable to breast feed her infant son George for whom a foster mother had to be found.

The George MacDonalds lived in a house in Duke Street at the corner of Church Street, built by George himself. Here their two eldest sons Charles and George were born in 1823 and 1824. A plaque marks the house today. It is now a dental surgery. Isabella MacDonald, by now a widow of sixty-eight, lived in the house next door on the corner of Church Street. There was a short passage and communicating door linking the two houses, a feature which MacDonald incorporated into his book *Robert Falconer* when the boy Robert sees Mary St John at the top of the stairs in her nightdress like 'an angel unawares'.

The MacDonalds were a close knit family and George, being for the first two years of his life in close proximity to his grandmother, must have formed an early relationship with her. She was probably as zealous in seeking his soul's salvation as she had been with her own children, insisting on attendance at the strictly calvinistic Missionar Church and the learning of the Shorter Catechism. But this did not have the desired effect upon her impressionable grandson. The apparent callousness of the calvinistic doctrine of predestination which was content to accept the relegation of vast numbers of souls into everlasting perdition, could not in his mind be squared with the love of God shown him by his parents, irrespective of his childish sins and so, like Robert Falconer, George worked out his own plan of salvation. In a moving passage, Robert Falconer describes to his scandalised Grannie how, when seated as one of the elect at the Supper of the Lamb, he will call upon all present, with Christ's permission, to take upon them the sins and suffering of their friends and relations who are in hell: 'We hae nae merit an' they hae nae merit and what for are we here and them there?' In the meantime like Robert he decided to concentrate on the second commandment as the first was too high for him and strove to love his neighbour as himself.

MacDonald's memories of the time in Duke Street must have been few but he had one clear memory from this period, his 'earliest definable memory' as he told his son Greville, when at the age of two he was taken to watch the funeral procession of the fourth Duke of Gordon. He saw the cortege winding its slow progress through Huntly on the way to Elgin — numerous black carriages drawn by horses with nodding plumes. It was a sad day for the people of Huntly for the Duke had been their friend, allocating to them smallholdings which would provide them with a living for themselves and their families. But now there would be no one to oppose the factors seizing their crofts and adding them to larger estates and turning out the cotters, many of whom were obliged to emigrate. When MacDonald grew up, he felt deeply about this injustice as the theme of his novel *What's Mine's Mine* illustrates. A whisky magnate from England buys up an estate previously administered by a local laird and ejects many of the poor tenants forcing them to emigrate to Canada.

George MacDonald senior and his brother James had been building a house on their recently acquired land at Pirriesmill. It was a plain, stone-built cottage, typically Scottish in style, built on three floors, solid and well constructed and in keeping with the characters of its builders. The first floor is partly below ground and steep steps lead up to the front door. In the roof there is an attic which at one time must have served George as a bedroom; he flew his kite through its sky-light. The house, at first called Bleachfield Cottage on account of its situation, was later always known as The Farm. It is still standing today and appears to be in as good a state of repair as when it was built one hundred and fifty years ago. The cottage faces north west on the two acre site with the river Bogie flowing not

13

far below and the bleaching fields between. Behind the house are hills, Corsiestane and Corvichen and more distantly to the west, the mound of Clashmach Hill. When the MacDonalds first moved into The Farm the surrounding land was bare, but this they soon remedied by planting saplings, in a circle all round the house. Today they have grown into great trees giving protection from the strong winds blowing from the north. But George MacDonald remembers in a nostalgic letter to his sister Bella how the wind 'howled in the chimney, against the windows and down at the kitchen door.'

The farm housed the families of both the MacDonald brothers and as the number of children increased there was barely enough room. Yet owing to the affectionate forbearance of the two and their complete rapport with each other there seems to have been no friction. After the move four more boys were born to George and Helen — James and John MacKay who both died as young children and Alexander and John Hill. James had two children, Frank and Margaret. There was also a servant girl called Bell Mavor. All Helen MacDonald's children were devoted to their mother and her death in 1832 when George was only eight must have brought great sadness to the household. In MacDonald's largely autobiographical novel, *Ranald Bannerman's Boyhood,* the mother is remembered as very beautiful and gentle and holding his head to her bosom when she was dying. He probably felt sorrier for his father than for himself for, affectionate and sensitive as he was, he had great powers of resilience.

For the next seven years the children were cared for by their mother's sister, Christina MacKay. She showed them love and affection and they were able to lead normal happy lives until in 1839 when George was fifteen their father married again. His second wife was Margaret McColl of Edinburgh. From this marriage came three daughters — Isabella, Louisa and Jane. Though fond of his sisters, George was not so close to them as to his brothers, as by the time they were of companionable age he had left Huntly for the south. But with Bella the eldest he had a special relationship, writing to her regularly during the period leading up to her death from tuberculosis when she was only twelve.

14

Margaret McColl was to win the affection of all her step-sons. George MacDonald himself held her in the greatest love and respect throughout his life. He predeceased her by five years for she died in 1910 at the age of one hundred and two.

A Country Boyhood

For the MacDonald brothers, boyhood was a happy time. George had a love of nature, an affinity with all creatures and a horror of cruelty. This he had inherited from his father who deplored grouse shooting and hunting stags. To George the very earth itself seemed to have a share with him in the hope of resurrection to eternal life. The ploughed field revealed this secret as he observes in his poem 'The Hidden Life':

There the slain sod lay, patient for grain
Turning its secrets upwards towards the sun
And hiding in a grave green sun-born grass
And daisies dipped in carmine; all must die
That others live and they arise again.

The Farm and its surroundings was an ideal place for young boys to grow up in. The river, the fields, the woods and more distantly the hills, in spring covered with nutty scented gorse, and in autumn purple heather, all provided a playground for the growing lad. MacDonald describes his home and how he felt about it in some lines from a poem called 'The Hills' which have a distinctly Wordsworthian flavour:

Behind my father's house there lies
A little grassy brae
Whose face my childhood's busy feet
Ran often up in play,
Whence on the chimneys I looked down
In wonderment alway.
Around the house where'er I turned
Great hills closed up the view.
The town midst their converging roots
Was clasped by rivers two.

17

From one hill to another sprang
The sky's great arch of blue.
It was a joy to climb their sides
And in the heather lie.
The bridle on my arm did hold
The pony feeding by.
Beneath, the silver streams, above
The white clouds in the sky.

It was not all play however. There was plenty of work to be done, but for the most part it was enjoyable. George MacDonald senior, and his brother James, while still retaining the bleaching factory had taken on dairy farming as well, with a view to using lactic acid in the whey as an essential ingredient for bleaching. When the bleaching business began to decline the farm produce still earned the family a useful income. There were thatched farm buildings at a little distance from the house where horses and cattle were kept. All the farm animals were dearly loved by the boys and even the cows seem to have been family pets with names like Hornie and Brownie.

The water-mill used in the bleaching process, as vividly described in *Robert Falconer* was later adapted for manufacturing potato flour and starch, an early concoction similar to arrowroot and called Farina. But the potato famine of the 1840s put an end to this industry.

Many of MacDonald's books are autobiographical. His son Greville MacDonald believed that 'to know in what full way the child is father of the man, we must study all his Scottish stories.' For first hand accounts of his childhood activities we can refer to *Robert Falconer, Alec Forbes* and *Ranald Bannerman's Boyhood*. George loved horses and one in particular – a grey mare called Missy. She was a beautiful creature with clean sinewy limbs and very agile, but so gentle that he could lie on her back and read a book while Missy grazed quietly along. Missy was also the name given to Robert Bannerman's fictional mare.

The MacDonalds grew oats and barley and George delighted in watching the plough-horse at work. In the summer he joined in the hay-making and later helped with the harvest. It was fun to ride the horses at watering time to drink at the trough by the pump, and to ride them home when the day's work was done, and what could have been more fascinating than to watch 'the grain dance from the sheaves under the skilful flails of the two strong men who belaboured them.'

The boys looked forward to the Saturday ritual of the linen bleaching. The supply of linen, accumulated during the week in the office under the gale room, was piled high on a broad-wheeled cart to be taken to the bleach fields. Like Robert and Shargar in *Robert Falconer* the boys climbed on the top of the linen and made a triumphal progress through the town from the factory to the mill. After going through a rigorous process of washing in the wauk-mill 'with the water splashing and squirting from the blows of their heels, the beatles thundering in arpeggio upon the huge cylinder round which the white cloth was wound', the linen was eventually flushed through a canal and flung on the green expanse of the well-mown grassy field, and secured with pegs. It billowed in the wind 'sometimes like sea-waves frozen and enchanted flat, seeking to rise and wallow in the wind with conscious depth and whelming mass'. In exchange for the ride the boys were expected to give some help. This they quite enjoyed, and when they were released there was the Bogie river flowing past their feet, its shallow waters alive with trout, inviting them to fish or swim.

At the lower end of the field, where the river had been dammed by a weir of large stones to form a mill-race, there was a deep pool. Into this they would plunge. Ranald Bannerman recalls the experience: 'O the summer days, with the hot sun drawing the odours from the feathery larches of the white-stemmed birches, when getting out of the water, I would lie in the warm soft grass where now and then the tenderest little breeze would creep over my skin, until the sun baking me more than was pleasant, I would rouse myself with an effort and running down to the fringe of rushes that bordered the full-brimmed river, plunge again headlong into the quiet brown water and dabble and swim till I was once more weary. For innocent animal delight I know of nothing to match those days — so warm, so pure-aired, so clean, so glad'.

As he lay on his back gazing up into the sky, an intense blue, flecked with white clouds, George experienced his first communing with nature. Its humanity smote his heart, 'its divinity entered his soul' and a strange indefinable longing possessed his spirit, a yearning which throughout his life would never wholly pass away.

Money was hard to come by in the MacDonald family and pocket-money non-existent, so the boys had to rely on their own resources. They made a kite, a 'dragon' with a long flying tail. They took great pains with its construction, collecting materials from various sources: a hoop or gird from the coopers, a slip of wood from the wright, cross pieces of folded paper for the tail and a length of string. The kite was over six feet in length and was a symbol of their boyhood. When George grew up and was done with childish things he let it float away through the sky-light of the attic where he slept.

When they were older the boys made a boat. Alec Forbes and Willie McWha in *Alec Forbes* launched theirs, the Bonnie Annie, in somewhat inauspicious circumstances: the river was in spate at the time and the boat got caught in the swirling waters of the mill-race. Miraculously however it survived to give pleasure to Alec and his friends for many hours. There is the hallmark of first hand experience in MacDonald's description of the joy of unmooring the boat and floating down the Bogie in the moonlight. Alec 'became aware then of a certain stillness pervading the universe, a stillness ever broken by the cries of eager men, ever closing and returning with gentleness not to be repelled, seeking to enfold and penetrate with its own healing, the minds of the noisy children of the earth'.

George loved riding. In the school holidays his father would permit him to take Missy, the grey mare and ride with his cousin Frank, Uncle James' son, over the moors for recreation and pure pleasure. They rode long distances over to Clashmach, Fondlans and Gartley hills, and also to the Binn which was still moorland. It had not yet been planted by the Forestry Commission.

These were the joys of summer, but winter was savage in Strathbogie. Snow covered the hills and often the lowlands too. The rivers were frozen and when the thaw came the water overflowed the banks causing wide-spread flooding. At Huntly there was danger of the two rivers between which it lay both bursting their banks at the same time and joining forces to overwhelm the little town. The inhabitants of The Farm, which stood on rising ground beyond the river would have had a full view of a flood's enormity such as the great one of 1829. In *Alec Forbes*, such a scene is vividly described. The characters in the novel felt 'separated from the opposite country by an impassable gulf.... Past them swept trees torn up by the roots...sheaves and trees went floating by. Then a cart with a drowned horse between the shafts in the central roll of the water... next came a great water wheel.'

But the frosty or snowy weather was full of delights for George and his brothers — lying in wait with a load of snowballs for unsuspecting school-fellows trudging through white uncharted lanes. It was an enchanted world, 'every branch every twig was laden with its sparkling burden of down-flickered flakes and threw long lovely shadows on the smooth featureless dazzle below'. When a hard black frost set in there was skating on the ice-bound waters of the Bogie and Deveron. The boys then lost no time in strapping on their iron studded boots and rough skates to skim over the glassy floor. It was exhilarating but it was not such fun for travellers. Snow storms as in *Castle Worlock* could render stage coaches immobile for several weeks.

In cold weather the smithy was a popular place. One could see the glowing fire through the open door and hear it roaring as the smith applied the bellows. He was an impressive and somewhat alarming figure clothed in a leather apron with huge bare brawny arms and a red face blackened with the fire, who made the sparks fly. There were strings of horses' shoes hanging nearby. Sometimes he would pick up a great iron spoon and dipping it in water would pour some on the fire which hissed in protest. Then he would pull out from the fire the huge iron bar now red hot and beat it on the anvil till the sparks flew up. There was a warm seat to be had by the fire for those the smith favoured. Here Alec Forbes brought young Annie Anderson to get warm when she was frozen through watching the boys build their boat.

A few hundred yards from The Farm was Ba'hill or Ball Hill, the traditional site of clan skirmishes in days gone by, and so called according to Ranald Bannerman because in one such combat the victors had afterwards played football with the heads of the vanquished! It was rough wild country covered with bilberry bushes, cranberries and dwarf junipers; they grew between the young pine trees which had recently been planted. In late summer George and his friends would make expeditions to pick the fruit. They also made raids on wild bees' nests in the stone walls, making off with pieces of honey-comb. On other occasions they roamed further afield over the heather-clad moors and hills, exploring the little streams and burns which bubbled out of the hillside or lay in the peat cutting, forming bracken-fringed pools. The boys liked to think these were inhabited by Kelpies. For George in retrospect, these expeditions were full of nostalgia. In after years the scent of the damp earth, or burning peat, or white clover and the perfumed breath of cows would bring the memory of the scenes of his childhood flooding back.

Sometimes the boys were taken to the sea for a change of air at Portsoy or Cullen. It is probable that some of the MacDonald family were still living in these places as the Piper of Culloden had had many children. The sea held a fascination for George and at one time he was resolved to be a sailor. The great attraction of Portsoy was the sea-bathing. A letter from George to his father from Portsoy at the age of ten, states that his cousin William is teaching him to swim. It is a wonder that he was not put off the sea by being made to drink salt water daily for his health's sake. George was delicate with a tendency to pleurisy and tuberculosis. They also went to Banff where their mother's brother George Mackay lived and their cousin Helen who was destined to play a significant part in MacDonald's life by introducing him to his future wife. Collecting the attractive Portsoy marbles was another pleasure, and exploring the caves along the coast. George also visited Fordyce, the one time home of his grandfather, and went into the castle, Cullen House, which may have provided the model for the Marquis of Lossie's home in *Malcolm*. The highlight of the holiday seems to have been a trip with William in a Prussian schooner and returning in the pilot boat. A fog crept up which made the transference from schooner to pilot boat the more exciting.

It might be assumed that with so much freedom to roam the countryside discipline was lax in the MacDonald household. This was far from the case. All the boys had been well brought up by their gentle mother to be polite, a system carried on by their aunt after her death, and all the time administered with a firm but kindly hand by their father. When George MacDonald senior re-married, his new wife Margaret appears to have been extremely impressed by the boys' good manners.

There was a particularly warm relationship between George and his father both in childhood and later life. As regards the early period, there is evidence of this in *Ranald Bannerman's Boyhood* where Ranald's clergyman father is possibly a portrait of George's own father. He was quite a gentle man – rather solemn but Ranald attributed that to the early death of his wife. He was seldom angry and rarely punished his children. His parishioners were devoted to him as he no doubt was to them, but he was above all loving to his children who trusted in him no matter what trouble they were in. Ranald remembered especially the bible stories he used to read to them after dinner on Sunday or when they were in bed at nights. He told them dramatically and made the stories live. Ranald's father expected obedience from his children and was severe in the case of lying, cruelty or injustice. When Ranald disgraced himself by throwing a stone at a little girl with the deliberate intention of hurting her, and tried to smoke an old lady out of her cottage by putting a lighted faggot through her letter-box, he felt bitterly ashamed and could not rest till he had confessed to his father and received forgiveness. Mr Bannerman took Ranald personally to apologise to the old dame and regarded the matter very seriously. But he gave his boys freedom because like Mr Walton in *The Seaboard Parish* he wanted them 'to be a law unto themselves'.

In later years George expressed his relationship with his father in the dedication of his pastoral poem 'The Hidden Life':

Thou hast been faithful to my highest need;
And I thy debtor ever, evermore,
Shall never feel the grateful burden sore;

> Yet most I thank thee, not for any deed,
> But for the sense thy living self did breed,
> Of fatherhood still at the great world's core.

George loved his father and thought him the best man in the world. His relationship with him can be likened to that of Wilfrid Cumbermede, in the book of that name, with his uncle. He felt him 'as a pure benevolence about and around him'. Although George MacDonald senior's devotion to God was paramount, his love for his children was profound.

His devout if bigoted mother had brought him up as a Missionar, regularly attending the Congregational Church of which Mr Hill was minister. He himself was a deacon and a great friend of the minister and used to go and pray with him every Monday, naming his youngest son John Hill after him. His religious views were mainly those of orthodox Calvinism, but in later life he did not condemn his son George's liberal ones and father and son amicably agreed to differ. Though serious minded, he had a great sense of humour. He had the misfortune to have his leg amputated below the knee and it had been replaced with a wooden one. Greville MacDonald in the biography of his father relates how charmingly MacDonald senior dismissed a group of protesters who, suspecting the MacDonalds were hoarding meal at The Farm in a time of famine, made an effigy of George and paraded it outside his house. George went out to meet them principally to quieten them as his wife was in confinement. Seeing the effigy he congratulated the men on the likeness but pointed out one fatal flaw. They had made the wrong leg wooden! The rebels appreciated the joke and went good-humouredly away. Shortly after the operation George had gone to stay with a friend near Banff where a noted minister was preaching. They attended the Church three times that Sunday and heard three sermons, each time on the same text 'The Lord taketh not pleasure in the legs of a man'!

George attended the Missionar Church regularly each Sunday, but like Ranald Bannerman he was not particularly impressed with the sermons. Even at an early age he could not reconcile his own idea of the love of God as experienced in that shown to him by his father, with selective salvation. He was conscious of an affinity with the universal spirit flowing through all created things and could not accept their relegation to external loss. 'I well remember feeling as a child I did not care for God to love me if he did not love everyone else' he wrote in *Weighed and Wanting*. Indeed he went so far as to hope with St Paul for the adoption of the whole creation. But if he could not accept his father's and his grandmother's brand of Calvinism, he was eager to adopt her passion for teetotalism. At the age of thirteen, much to his grandmother's delight, George became President of the Huntly Juvenile Temperance Society which was formed in 1837 and held in the MacDonald Thread Factory. Three years earlier he had shown strength of character in refusing some gin when offered some by his hostess.

When George was thirteen the Strathbogie Controversy was beginning. It was one of the chief factors contributing to the Disruption of the Church of Scotland in 1843. The question at issue concerned the manner in which ministers were to be appointed. The older method dating from 1712 was by patronage in which case a minister could be forced on a congregation against the people's will. The majority of presbyterians still upheld this method, but a minority supported the Veto Act, passed by the General Assembly of the Kirk in 1834 by which no minister could be given a living without the consent of the majority of male heads of families in the parish. The argument came to a head in the tiny village of Marnoch about midway between Huntly and Portsoy in the presbytery of Strathbogie. The candidate appointed by the Patron, the Earl of Fife, was rejected by the parishioners in accordance with the Veto Act. They accepted another nominee more to their taste. The rejected candidate meanwhile appealed to the Civil Court of Sessions and won his case, so Marnoch had two ministers for the next four years.

But the root cause of the conflict was the existence in the Presbyterian Church of two fundamentally opposing religious views. The moderates who supported patronage, tended to be more easy-going and wanted liberation from the sterner doctrines of the Church concerning sin, punishment and hell, and the condemnation of social

25

pleasures such as theatre-going and dancing; whereas the upholders of the Veto Act retained an austere attitude to religion, condemning most pleasures and demanding an exact obedience to the Ten Commandments. They believed in salvation for the elect only, and set great store by preaching which denounced sin and put the fear of everlasting punishment into a man's heart. They had also a strong belief in the efficacy of prayer for converting back-sliders and unbelievers.

George was of course too young at the time to be personally concerned in the dispute, but its sequel in the final Disruption of the Church in 1843 when one third of the ministers rebelled against the Patronage Act and formed a Church of Scotland wholly dependent on the financial support of their members, was to affect him deeply when he was a student at Aberdeen University. It is obvious that his grandmother would side with the stern Calvinists in rejecting the so-called enlightened views of the moderates, but then she had already rejected them in abandoning the Established Church for the Missionar Kirk where preaching was full of evangelising zeal based on uncompromising Calvinistic creeds and where the only guide to salvation for the young was the Shorter Catechism, as George was to remember to his cost at school.

Whether or not he was involved in the controversy at the time, it appears as a live issue in several of his novels. In *Alec Forbes* for example, an argument takes place between George McWha the father of Alec's friend Willie and Thomas Crann the mason. The first was a member of Muckle Kirk, and the second belonged to the Independent Missionar Church. George does his best to win Thomas over, but the latter dismisses the Parish Church as a place 'where we get but the dry bones o'morality'. George taunts him with not yet having a minister of their own and Thomas replies 'we're no like you — forced to swallow any jabble o' luke-warm water, that's been standin' in the sun frae years an' tae years en', just because the patron pleases to stick a pump into it an' call it a well o' salvation. We'll ken where the water comes frae — we'll taste them all and choose accordin'. On another occasion Alec finds himself at the Missionar Kirk being preached at by the fiery Mr Turnbull who begins by reading the curses on Mount Ebal and ends with a terrible denunciation of wrath upon the sinners who had been called and would not come. He prayed for those exposed to hell ... the smoke of whose torments would arise and choke the elect themselves about the throne of God — the hell of Exhausted Mercy (as Alec called it).

Another important tenet of the strict Calvinism with which MacDonald in later life could not agree was sabbatarianism. In *David Elginbrod* he expresses his opinion on the matter. Hugh Sutherland felt liberated when he turned into Regents Park on a Sunday and saw people enjoying themselves. He kept as far as possible from the rank of open-air preachers and was able to thank God that all the world did not keep 'Scotch Sabbath' — ' a day neither Mosaic nor Jewish nor Christian: not Mosaic in as much as it kills the very essence of the fourth commandment, which is Rest, transmuting it into what the chemists would call a mechanical mixture of service and inertia; not Jewish, in as much as it is ten times more severe and formal, and full of negations than that of the Sabbatarian Jews reproved by the Saviour for their idolatry of the day; and unchristian in as much as it elevates into an especial test of piety a custom not even mentioned by the founders of Christianity at all — that, namely, of accounting this day more holy than all the rest'. To this George MacDonald adds a rider of his own, between himself 'and the vision of the Lord's Day indeed there arises too often the nightmare memory of a Scotch Sabbath.... The great men and women whom I have known in Scotland seem to me, as I look back, to move about the mists of a Scotch Sabbath like a company of way-worn angels in the limbo of Vanity in which there is no air whereupon to smite their sounding wings that they may rise into the sunshine of God's presence.'

This religious controversy which resulted from the Veto Act of 1834 was just beginning when the MacDonald boys attended their first school. It was a long low thatched building in Bogie Street with a garret above which had once been a weaver's shed. There were five windows facing on the lane. The description of it in *Alec Forbes* is probably an accurate one, and the general set-up of the school can be gathered from the account of Annie Anderson's first day there.

The schoolmaster was the Revd Colin Stewart, a minister of the Parish Kirk. He was a typical disciplinarian of the day, a tyrant with sadistic tendencies, bent on proving the truth of the maxim 'Spare the rod and spoil the child' except that in his case it was the tawse or strap which he wielded. He is portrayed in *Alec Forbes* as the notorious Murdock Malinson, a Dickensian type of dominie with a savage sense of duty. All the pupils suffered at his hands, both boys and girls, yet strangely enough in *Alec Forbes*, George MacDonald defends the use of corporal punishment, and to a certain extent justifies the master in its use. 'It was the custom of the time and of the country to use the tawse unsparingly. In the hands of a wise and even-tempered man no harm could result from the use of this instrument of justice, but in the hands of a fierce tempered and therefore changeable man of small moral stature and liable to prejudices and offence, it became the means of unspeakable injury to those under his care'.

One such indeed was his own younger brother James, described in *Alec Forbes* as 'a little pale-faced boy who blundered a good deal and in so doing received lash after lash of the cruel serpent of leather round his little thin legs'. George must have seen the blue wheals on his brother's legs when he was undressed for the night by his indignant aunt. James died when he was eight years old.

School began at 7 a.m. when Mr Stewart opened the school door and the children all trooped in to the two rows of double desks with a gangway between. The first item in the school procedure was prayer. While the master prayed the children stood in silence, but only their tongues were still; a fantastic display of dumb-show followed, but the master afraid of being himself detected in the attempt to combine prayer and vision, kept his eyelids screwed tight together and played the spy with his ears alone, and did not see the amazing performance as depicted in *Alec Forbes* 'of projected tongue, winking eyes, contorted features and wild use of hands and arms for the means of telegraphic despatches to all parts of the room', which continued throughout the ceremony.

Prayer was followed by bible reading for those who could read.

The rest did spelling. Throughout the day proceedings were punctuated by applications of the tawse, sometimes to the innocent as well as the guilty.

There is no evidence that Stewart repented of his cruelty, but in *Alec Forbes* Malinson makes good by losing his life in an attempt to save from the great flood, a pupil whom after crippling him for life with his chastisement, he had befriended. Even in the portrayal of fictitious characters George MacDonald was loth to assign any soul to perdition.

School ended at 1 p.m. when the scholars returned home for dinner. It resumed at 3 p.m. and continued till 5 p.m. when the children were dismissed with another extempore prayer. On Saturday they learned the Shorter Catechism. Failure to do so resulted in the tawse or in their being kept in and left 'to chew the cud of ill-cooked theology'. One such occasion is described by MacDonald in *Alec Forbes* when Annie Anderson escaped through the window with Alec's help and fetched bread to feed the other hungry detainees. 'A succession of jubilant shouts usually arose as the boys rushed out into the lane. Every day to them was a cycle of strife, suffering and deliverance. Birth and death with the life struggle between, were shadowed out in it with this difference, that the God of a corrupt Calvinism in the person of Murdock Malinson, ruled the world and not the God revealed in the man Christ Jesus; and most of them having felt the day more or less a burden were now going home to heaven for the night'. This is evidently what home meant to George MacDonald.

In spite of their natural revulsion to the school and its master, the boys attended regularly, weather and health permitting. The school was about half a mile from The Farm on the far side of the Bogie, and sometimes in snowy weather the way was impassable. Then he was happy to stay at home and indulge his great love of reading, *Pilgrim's Progress*, Milton's *Comus* and *Paradise Lost*. But salvation was at hand. George MacDonald senior had long been dissatisfied with conditions at the Parish School and with Mr Stewart's regime. When the younger George was eleven his father took the law into his own hands and set up a school in McVeagh's old factory in MacDonald

Street and called it the Adventure School. The Rev Alexander Millar, son of the minister of the United Free Church in Huntly was appointed master. Under his tuition George began to make rapid progress, for Millar, realising the boy's potential, gave him every encouragement which included extra tuition. George used to join a class before breakfast and stay on afterwards and have breakfast of porridge and milk with the family of another pupil. Scottish schools have long had a high academic standard, boys from all walks of life being taught Latin, Greek, mathematics and sciences such as astronomy from an early age. George was soon writing verse. His metrical composition on the subject of patriotism caused quite a sensation. He was also given the opportunity to teach other children.

George would often go home with the master to read Vergil and Horace staying for supper of potatoes, milk, oat cake and butter, yet not without incurring the jealousy of some of the boys.

George gives a portrait of Alexander Millar in the character of Alexander Graham in *Malcolm*, and to a lesser degree in Mr Wilson, Ranald Bannerman's schoolmaster. Though ordained, Graham had no desire to be in charge of a parish or congregation. He was a gentle unassuming man with a great love of children. He was not married and had a housekeeper. His method of teaching was to present facts to the children and suggest both sides of an argument, and then let them think the matter out for themselves, stimulating the heart as well as the intellect. He rarely contradicted a pupil, but would oppose error only by teaching the truth. He made the children think by asking them the right questions. When he spoke of the things he loved best he became lyrical in his eloquence. Graham never used corporal punishment, but restrained his pupils by using for each a nickname appropriate to the individual's character. It was a sign of the master's respect and favour. But that special name could be forfeited if the pupil should fall from grace by fighting or dishonesty. Graham devised this unique method of maintaining discipline from the Book of Revelation. If this is a portrait of Alexander Millar it is obvious that he would be the ideal teacher for the young George MacDonald.

George was a well set up lad in spite of his delicacy. In later life his son Ranald remembers his father as 'broad-shouldered and long limbed and narrow flanked with the build of an athlete but with slender hands and feet. His face was strong-featured and his hair and beard thick and very black, but it was his eyes which were the most remarkable feature. They were deep set of a liquid blue as southern sea-water at rest, keen as a northern sky in cloudless frost at mid-day — the only eyes I have ever known with always a spark and sometimes a flash in them'. Yet in spite of his broad shoulders and long arms, as a boy George was no good at throwing, possibly owing to bronchial trouble, so when a fight was on with the boys of another school which happened not infrequently, he was given the job of collecting stones and missiles and supplying his comrades with them. Boy-like, George seems to have enjoyed the conflict which is graphically described in *Ranald Bannerman's Boyhood*. The opposing school acquired an engine of war in the shape of a builder's hand-waggon. On this the boys mounted and proceeded to hurtle down the hill towards their enemies who awaited them with a volley of stones. Unfortunately the waggon over-turned and Ranald's arch-enemy, Scroggie, broke his leg. George MacDonald's inability to throw was amply compensated for by the tremendous enthusiasm with which he entered the fray, a MacDonald fighting a Campbell, and he was soon acknowledged leader.

At one time George had a passion for the sea and was determined, if he could obtain his father's permission, to go to sea. He wrote to him accordingly, aged fourteen:

My Dear Father

It is now time for me to be thinking of what I should betake myself to and tho' I would be sorry to displease you in any way yet I must tell you that the sea is my delight and that I wish to go to it as soon as possible and I hope that you will not use your parental authority to prevent me, as you undoubtedly can. I feel I would be continually longing to be at sea.... O let me dear father for I could not be happy at anything else.... If it were not for putting you to too much trouble I would beg an answer in writing but I can hardly expect it though I much wish it.

Your affectionate son, George

His father was doubtful about what kind of a career would suit his second son, but he was resolved that he should have the best education possible. His eldest son Charles was already at Aberdeen University, and the family finances would not permit paying fees for George, so it would be necessary for him to be coached for a scholarship.

If *Robert Falconer* is autobiographical, George drove himself hard in his last year at his Huntly school. 'He gained permission from his grandmother [father] to remove his bed to the garret and there ... he would often rise at four in the morning, even when the snow lay a foot thick on the skylight, kindle his lamp by means of a tinder-box and a splinter of wood dipped in sulphur, and sitting down in the keen cold, turn half a page of Addison into something as near Ciceronian Latin as he could effect. This would take him an hour and a half to two hours, when he would tumble into bed blue and stiff, and sleep till it was time to get up and go to school before breakfast'.

At the age of sixteen George was sent to Aulton Grammar School in Aberdeen for the next stage of his education in preparation for the University, and to compete for a bursary.

Fond as he was of his home and his family he looked forward eagerly to the great adventure he was so soon to share with his elder brother. Through the experience of Robert Falconer, we can share his excitement as he stood with his trunk and tuck-box waiting for the scarlet Mail Coach to pick him up for the forty mile journey to Aberdeen. 'Long before the coach rounded the corner the post-horn rang out warning of its approach. It was his chariot of desire to carry him up to a heaven where all labour is delight. The four horses pulled up, the guard in his red livery descended from the box, his luggage was hoisted up, Robert scrambled to his seat, the horn blew and once again they were off'.

This is how George's boyhood ended and his new life began. The year was 1840.

College Days in Aberdeen

Aulton Grammar School in Old Aberdeen was regarded as a kind of preparatory school for the University. Dating back to the thirteenth century its foundation was believed to be one of the earliest in the country. The single story school which George MacDonald attended was built about 1757. It was situated in Schoolhill and continued in use until 1883 when a new building was provided. The poet Byron was at one time a pupil there. The teaching was rigorous and thorough especially in Latin which was then a vital subject for University entrance.

There were several other country lads at the school, sent like George to improve their standards, so he would have felt quite at home. When not engaged in their studies the boys enjoyed, as at home, the rough and tumble of the playground. Their animal spirits, according to Robert Falconer and Alec Forbes seem to have been in the same category as those of the boys in *Tom Brown's School Days*. Perhaps the playground invited horse-play. There was nothing else to do in 'a parallelogram of low stone walls, containing a roughly gravelled court'. There was plenty of shouting as the boys rushed to and fro with mad kicks of the football, action which not surprisingly often produced casualties. George joined in with vigour.

The country boy's first impressions of Aberdeen were mixed. The city itself with its long streets of brightly lit shops and the pavements as described in *Alec Forbes* 'filled with men and women moving in different directions like a double row of busy ants' must have been bewildering at first and a poor substitute for the rural peace of The Farm, but there was the compensation of the sea for which he had so much affection. George had lodgings in Spital Brae in the Old Town close to King's College and not far from the school. His room was an attic or garret in a two-storeyed house with a distant view of the sea. With no tower blocks intruding on the horizon as there are to-day, his attic window would have afforded an uninterrupted vista across fields and sand-hills to the slatey blue waters of the North Sea. His lodgings were modest and in keeping with the family's limited resources and he provided his own potatoes and oatmeal. There is an extant letter to his father asking for further supplies. Robert Falconer was provided with a tuck-box containing a linen bag of oatmeal, thick layers of oatcake, cheeses, butter and jam, but these last were luxuries.

The sea was George's life-line. When concentrated sessions of translating Livy or Vergil became too much of a burden 'he would fling down his dictionary or pen and fly in a straight line like a sea-gull, weary of lake and river down to the waste shore of the great deep' *(Robert Falconer)*. But he worked hard, anxious not to let his father down. He had often admired King's College from a distance. It was most impressive with its stone-crowned tower dating back to 1500; but now as he passed beneath its arch on the way to the Scholarship examination and crossed the quadrangle in the company of the other boys, it felt like the Day of Judgement especially when the black-gowned professors walked in. Then indeed a great awe fell upon the assembly. Robert Falconer had to turn a passage from Robertson's *History of Scotland* into Latin. It was about Mary Queen of Scots and afterwards he was upset to realise that in his translation he had made the Queen masculine!

In the examination George MacDonald was awarded the Fullarton Bursary at Kings College of fourteen pounds a year. Robert Falconer received only five pounds and had to enter for the scholarship a second time, but this was not George's own experience.

At the time when he entered College in 1840 there were two separate and distinct Universities. Marischal College was mainly for the sons of residents of Aberdeen, business men and the professional classes. It prepared students for careers such as medicine, law or the church, while King's College catered more for boys from country areas in the North East of Scotland and the Western Highlands. George's contemporaries were a mixed company and some were sons of crofters, ploughmen or shop-keepers, country bumpkins smelling of fields and the farm-yard, 'shock-headed lads with much of the looks and manners of year old bullocks, mostly with freckled faces and a certain general irresponsiveness of feature'. Others were sons of the landed gentry, old Highland families whose ancestors had administered their land as lairds for generations. George could tell the aristocracy by their general bearing as well as the cut of their clothes and distinctive neckerchiefs. He himself really came in between these two categories. His clothes, though plain were clean and neat and his manners more civilised than those of his crofter brethren. For the most part it was a healthy social mix with only a few students giving themselves airs and not wishing to associate with the multitude.

George MacDonald must have felt thrilled when he traversed the path beneath the arch and tower with crown of stone for the second time, but now as a Bejan or 'fresh man' wearing his scarlet gown. The curriculum at Kings was a general one — it was part of a structured four year course which included Latin, Greek, Mathematics, Moral Philosophy, Natural Philosophy and Chemistry. Mrs Forbes was content to let Alec go to the University because the curriculum was common to all professions — no narrow specialisation — and he would make no worse a farmer for having an A.M. after his name. However, there was some choice of subject in addition to the basic course. In a letter to his father in 1841 George is wondering whether to take chemistry and later philosophy. His chief interest at this time seemed to be in literature. He learned German so as to have access to German literary and philosophical writers. But his interests were not purely studious. He enjoyed debating and attended classes organized by the Magistrande or Fourth year students and it was not long before he was taking part. An incident is related in *Alec Forbes* which suggests that the Senior Students rather looked down on the Bejans or Yellow Beaks, calling them clod-hoppers who had just 'come from herding their fathers' cows', and who could express themselves only in bovine language.

George's scientific aspirations were not yet to be realised. After completing only the first and second years of the course he was summoned home and informed by his father that it was no longer possible to maintain him at College and to meet the expenses which the bursary could not cover. By 1842, the year in which he should have begun his third session, crofters in the Highlands and the North East of Scotland were experiencing great financial hardship and this affected conditions at The Farm. Small farmers were finding it increasingly difficult to compete against large farms where machinery was in use. There was also an influx of cheap grain from abroad which the Corn Laws, not yet repealed, were ineffective in stemming. The day of the small farmer and private enterprise was coming to a close and cottage industries such as spinning and weaving were also threatened. With these troubles as well as the ever-present burden of having to pay off their brother's debt to the bank, George MacDonald senior and his brother James were in a state of financial crisis. So George came home.

It was customary for poor students from crofts and villages in the surrounding countryside to take on agricultural work for seven months of the year in order to augment their meagre income and pay for their tuition. In spring they followed the plough and in autumn reaped the harvest. At College they provided their own food in the shape of oatmeal, potatoes and other vegetables. Often, like Robert Falconer's college friend Eric Ericson, they went hungry and their health was affected. For not only did they have to do hard manual work on the land but could not afford coach fares, so had sometimes to walk a hundred miles or more to find work, often on an empty stomach with blistered feet and their stockings all in holes. Sometimes they travelled in groups and were put up at an Inn, The Boar's Head or the Gordon Arms or whatever it might be.

These students were mainly from the cottar class, feudal dependants with an acre or two of land in return for which they worked hard for the laird. In George MacDonald's opinion they were the salt of the earth, God-fearing and living in close-knit family groups, loyal to their land and to their superior. But they were a dying race. Gradually their farms failed or were swallowed up in larger ones and emigration was the only solution. Yet by their steadfastness they had a contribution to make wherever they went. 'If Scotland is worse the world is better'. With this thought MacDonald consoled himself for their passing.

George MacDonald's health was not sufficiently robust for him to take up work on the land for any length of time, yet it was necessary for him to contribute to the family's support. The employment which he eventually found for the summer of 1842, cataloguing a library at some great house or castle in the far north of Scotland, proved more delightful and rewarding than he could possibly have imagined and was to have far-reaching results in shaping his future career. In no fewer than five of his books a library is an important setting for the action of the plot. In *Lilith* for example, Vane's romantic and mystical adventure begins and ends in the library of a mansion. Wilfrid Cumbermede found the secret of his inheritance while cataloguing the books at Moldwarp Hall and discovered that 'books themselves repay him for the trouble he takes in arranging them'. The unwitting discovery by Donal Grant of the most macabre and gruesome crime imaginable, came from his double role of tutor and librarian at Castle Graham. Donal longed to work in a great library, to feast on the thoughts of men, but he found instead an heroic adventure which was to change the course of his life. Duncan in *The Portent* asked to catalogue the books in a library where he was staying, because he regarded books as a kind of sacrament 'as indeed what on God's earth is not'. His task of arranging the books was often delayed as he discovered fascinating romances and 'a nest of German Classics'.

The identity of George's library cannot unfortunately be established. Alec Forbes' colleague Cupples, who was connected with the College library, referred to a 'grit leebrary i' the far north', and the Revd Robert Troup who married George's cousin Margaret, the daughter of his Uncle James, declared that George had definitely referred to this interlude in his University education. Assuming this to be the fact, Greville MacDonald suggests two possible libraries: Thurso Castle in Caithness, now alas a ruin, but at that time the property of Sir George Sinclair whose father Sir John had been a collector of German literature, such as had delighted Duncan in *The Portent*. Before his death in 1835, Sir John had been a patron of the MacDonald family's patent potato flour called Farina. This shows that the MacDonalds had some acquaintance with the Sinclair family. A less likely alternative perhaps, is Dunbeath Castle also in Caithness on the North East coast, which at that time was reputed to have had a wonderful library. The suggestion was made by the wife of the then owner, Lady Alexander Sinclair. In either case the far north is an apt description.

MacDonald's sojourn in the library increased his knowledge of literature in general and he became acquainted with the poetry of the sixteenth century. At first it seems to have been in the poets that his chief interest lay, but when he discovered German romantic writers, his enthusiasm knew no bounds. It is impossible to say precisely what the works were which inspired him so much. Greville MacDonald believes one to have been A.E.T. Hoffman's *Golden Pot* which George MacDonald more than once enthuses about and recommends as thoroughly worthwhile reading. Hoffman's romantic stories not only provided the inspiration for Offenbach's fantastic light opera *The Tales of Hoffman* but in later years for MacDonald's own fairy tale, *Phantastes* and others such as *The Princess and the Goblin, At the Back of the North Wind* and *Lilith*. In all of these much of the action takes place in a world behind the world which is painted more vividly and where truth may be more easily perceived. In these 'faery' romances there is no labouring of a moral; the action through the medium in which it is expressed speaks for itself. In the library George MacDonald may also have discovered Novalis, the pen-name of the German romantic poet and novelist F.L. von Hardenberg, whose *Twelve Spiritual Songs* MacDonald was ten years later to translate from the German. He felt a special affinity with the poet's mystical approach to death and human loss.

George MacDonald's literary experiences in that remote Scottish library not only played a great part in developing his most distinctive genre — the contribution to our British literature for which he is best remembered and most valued — the influence which stemmed from his literary excursion in 'the grit leebrary' was more far-reaching yet. Some literary giants of more recent times have acknowledged their debt to MacDonald's 'faerie' romances, namely members of the Inklings at Oxford — Tolkein, Charles Williams and above all C.S. Lewis who regarded him as his master. Lewis was already steeped in romanticism when he discovered *Phantastes* but it was not the romanticism of it which attracted him but rather 'a sort of cool morning innocence'. He declared that *Phantastes* stimulated and purified his imagination and as a result of this baptism the tales of *Narnia, Perelandra, The Pilgrim's Regress* and *The Great Divorce* were born.

Yet it was not as a man of letters that Lewis revered MacDonald but rather as a Christian teacher. It is true that in the preface to the anthology he declares that as a myth maker 'MacDonald is the greatest genius of this kind I know' but Lewis was able to come to this conclusion because he believed that the essence of a myth was contained in its content rather than in its form. Myth making therefore came in his opinion 'outside the criteria usually applied to a species of literary art'. G.K. Chesterton, also a great admirer of MacDonald who in his preface to Greville MacDonald's biography of his parents *George MacDonald and his Wife* confesses that MacDonald 'made a difference to my whole existence' holds a similar view regarding the effect his writing makes upon the reader: it 'depends rather on a sympathy with the substance than on the first sight of the form'.

As a writer Lewis could in fact grant his master a place neither in the first or second rank but wisdom and holiness spoke to him from all MacDonald's writing. In the Fantasies this influence is especially evident. 'I had not the faintest notion what I had let myself in for by trying *Phantastes*' Lewis tells his readers in his autobiography *Surprised by Joy* 'but I saw the bright shadow coming out of the book into the real world and resting there, transforming all common things and yet itself unchanged'. The 'bright shadow' was joy.

Even in the novels which Chesterton describes as 'uneven' and 'rather too full' and which Lewis admits have 'intolerable faults', after reading *Wilfrid Cumbermede* he could discover 'hidden nuggets of gold of so fine a quality that it carries off the dross'.

George returned to Aberdeen for the 1834-44 session with a new enthusiasm for his studies. His interests now were wider. He had already learned German which stood him in good stead when he came to tackle the German classics which impressed him so much. On his return he applied himself to the study of chemistry, a subject which he had probably had little to do with at school where laboratory facilities did not exist. His interest in the sciences derived from a natural curiosity about how things work, but as he himself in later life was to admit, scientific explanations rob nature of its magic and leave the world the poorer. George's acquaintance with chemistry led to an ambition to take up Medicine. For humanitarian reasons, as expressed by Robert Falconer, he hankered after the opportunities such a profession would afford. There was plenty of poverty to be seen in the streets of Aberdeen and George did what he could, through Blackfriars Street Congregational Church which he attended, to better the lot of the poor; by teaching in Sunday School and helping the minister, the Revd John Kennedy with the School of Industry. It catered for eight hundred children, providing a meal for them every day. George had been used to poverty in Huntly; his grandmother had adopted two orphans, but he had never before seen so much deprivation and squalor.

It was probably lack of funds which initially prevented him from fulfilling his ambition to become a doctor. He compensated for this later however, by assigning Robert Falconer to the medical profession and following his career as a great-hearted, devoted physician striving to improve social conditions in the slums of London. It must have been a cause of happiness to him too, that his eldest son Greville was able to follow the profession which he himself was denied. In 'A Hidden Life' a poem dedicated to his father and written in 1857 in which he eulogizes the lot of the poor scholar-ploughman who died of consumption at an early age, he philosophises regarding the temptation to imagine that only philanthropic works on a grand scale are worthy of his gifts

the world is in God's hand
this part of it is mine.
…All crowds are made of individuals

...I cannot throw
A mass of good into the general midst
Whereof each man may seize a private share.

George MacDonald was not always serious. He enjoyed the social life the University provided. He was an impressive speaker in debates, he joined in charades especially when they involved dressing up. He was not without vanity and often appeared in flamboyant clothing. A fellow student remembered him wearing a tartan coat, 'the most dazzling affair in dress I ever saw a student wear'. Even in later life he had a romantic attachment to Highland dress. In Scotland he would have passed unnoticed, but in London he looked distinguished, if a trifle eccentric, with tartan plaid, white shirt front and scarlet cravat, his hair and beard long and flowing. George's son Ranald remembers him in a 'gorgeous smoking jacket and cap, a waist coat with numerous gilt buttons and elegant boots and shoes'. In summer he wore a white serge suit.

At College George was generally sought after as good company although at times he appeared withdrawn and detached. A kind of melancholy introspection would descend upon him and he felt the need to escape and express his thoughts in verse. At such times the sea drew him like a magnet. Throughout his college career George wrote poetry although not of very great quality. He was experimenting with metres, while all the time ideas were struggling for expression. One poem from this period written in blank verse called 'David', showed promise. This is interesting as it was to be the medium in which his most successful poems 'The Hidden Life' and 'Within and Without' were written.

MacDonald shared his aspirations with his cousin Helen Mackay, who was soon to marry his future wife's brother Alexander Powell. He gave her a notebook containing some of his poems. They had a happy relationship, Helen teasing George when he became too serious. But there was plenty to be serious about for a University student in those days. It was a time for change and unrest in both religion and politics. George concerned himself with both.

There was much discussion about the aims of Chartism: the demands of universal suffrage for men, election of Members of

41

Parliament by ballot and the opportunity for members to be elected from any class of society. George was always ready to champion the under-dog and at the same time he felt that it was time that the interests of minority groups like the crofters should be represented in Parliament. But for him it was basically a wider issue; the rights of the individual were at stake and this was a religious matter as well as a political one. If there was no equality for the children of God according to Calvinism, why should there be in politics a fair deal for all? This was a question which he must have put to himself. Subconsciously MacDonald had from childhood felt a revulsion towards the idea of predestination and the literal interpretation of the bible on which it is based. At Aberdeen he had dutifully attended with his brother the Congregational Church because it was similar to the one in which he had been brought up. Nor did he wish to grieve his father to whom strict Calvinism meant so much. But a wind of change was blowing in Aberdeen and throughout Scotland which was akin to the spirit of George MacDonald.

In Glasgow students who supported the Doctrine of Universal Redemption were expelled from their theological College. In 1841 the Revd James Morison left the Congregational Secession Church in protest against the doctrine of salvation for the elect only, and in 1843 he and other Morisonians formed the Evangelical Union. This further disharmony — it did not amount to a split from the established Church of Scotland — created an atmosphere of dissatisfaction and uncertainty amongst young people in general, especially in students, part of whose vocation it is to ponder and query. Several young men in Blackfriars Congregational Church in particular, including George MacDonald, were affected. One of his chief objections to the church as he had experienced it was the way in which ministers blackmailed and tyrannised their congregations by emphasising dogma at the expense of the Gospel, a criticism which he levelled at other religious denominations too. He sincerely believed that a man must live by the message he received personally from his knowledge of the Gospel through his own conscience, not by someone elses interpretation of it. As a Child of God the individual has a unique vision of the will of God, and so therefore does everyone else. In 'The Disciple', a poem published in 1868, he recalls how he felt during his student days:

> Old books new facts they preach aloud
> Their tones like wisdom fall:
> I see a face amid the crowd
> Whose smile were worth them all.

MacDonald found several kindred spirits among his fellow students. Some were of the same intellectual stature as himself: William Geddes, the Greek scholar, later Principal of the University, Alexander Roberts one of the translaters of the revised version of the New Testament, and J. Robert Troup who eventually married his cousin Margaret MacDonald. Troup, after a period of preparation for the Congregational Ministry at Highbury College, London, became John Hill's assistant Minister at Huntly. There were also several young students who attended Blackfriars Street Church who used to gather together weekly with him for a meal and discussion. MacDonald had also the moral support and companionship of his brother Charles, a year his senior, who during the last year of George's time at College was in business. The brothers shared lodgings. But he does not seem to have enjoyed any close friendship such as Alec Forbes' relationship with Cupples and Robert Falconer's with Ericson, but the importance to Alec and Robert of these attachments suggests that there may have been. There is no record either of George MacDonald enjoying much female society at College. Yet again Alec's beautiful cousin Kate looms large in his life and his loss of her love and subsequent death affected him deeply. Could there perhaps be some connection between Kate and George's dearly loved cousin Helen Mackay whose marriage to Alexander Powell took place in 1844 during George's last year at College?

George MacDonald retained his own vision of life intact throughout University days. He had the inner integrity to safeguard and nurture something within him that amounted to more than intellectual curiosity and he was aware of this in himself. Indeed as he makes clear in one of his early poems, he felt this detachment from the world too:

I sit and gaze from window high
Upon the noisy street
No part in this great coil have I,
No fate to go and meet.

My books long days have untouched lain,
The lecture hour is slow,
For other thoughts go through my brain,
Than those gowned bosoms know.

This sense of standing apart from the world and university extended to the very core of his existence and in a religious context, he gives expression to this feeling:

My story, too, thou knowest, God,
Is different from the rest;
Thou knowest — none but thee — the load,
With which my heart is pressed.

George MacDonald took his M.A. in 1845 and left the University without any clear ideas as to what he should do.

Highbury and Arundel

Although George MacDonald had left College without any definite career in view he had not entirely given up the idea of the ministry, but honesty prevented him from making a firm decision. He longed to evangelise, yet how could be preach a gospel about which, in its accepted Calvinist form, he had serious reservations? At the same time his University education had proved that his natural bent was academic rather than practical which narrowed the field of possible careers for a young man from his background.

MacDonald had already done some tutoring during his vacations. He taught the two sons of a Presbyterian minister at Banff. So when a friend of his father, the Revd John Morison, now a fashionable preacher in the Trevor independent chapel in Brompton informed him of a vacancy for the post of tutor to a family in his congregation living in Fulham, it seemed a solution, if only a temporary one, to the problem. So George MacDonald left home for London. His experiences as a tutor do not seem to have been particularly happy. He found his pupils, three small boys and two noisy girls, dull, unresponsive and spoilt. There was little freedom and he disliked the compulsory attendance with his charges at chapel twice every Sunday. Conditions in the house were uncongenial, the food was meagre, his health was uncertain and he had no room in which to study. Like Hugh Sutherland in *David Elginbrod*, he would emerge from a period of reading, blue with cold. Fortunately he was able to find relief from the monotony of his duties by visiting his cousin Helen Mackay, now married to Alexander Powell and living at Stamford Grove, Upper Clapton. She lost no time in introducing him to the other members of her husband's family.

The Powells lived in a large rambling Georgian house called The Limes. It had good stabling and a garden of three-quarters of an acre. The house needed to be large as James Powell and his wife had thirteen children though five died young. Of the surviving ones only two were boys. They were a pious family belonging to the Congregational Church, but lively and intelligent and full of affection for each other. The father James Powell was strict in his religious views and thought the theatre wicked but he enjoyed playing the violin. He was a prosperous business man in the leather trade, and an excellent book binder which he regarded as a hobby, and he was very generous. He took a liking to George immediately, indeed the whole family gave him a warm welcome and The Limes became to him a home from home. George made himself useful to the household. He advised the girls about their reading matter, recommending and reading Tennyson and Wordsworth with them. He taught the youngest girl, Angela, to read. She was probably dyslectic and though naturally intelligent was labelled stupid by her elder sisters. He also concerned himself with the philanthropic aspirations of Phoebe the second sister and he had various protégées of his own in London whom he tried to help out of his meagre stipend. But it was to the third daughter Louisa, that George felt irresistibly drawn and the attraction appears to have been mutual. Louisa was soon teaching him to sew and mend his clothes, and embroider. As a result of this in the year 1846 he was able to work a pair of embroidered slippers for his step-mother. Another sign of the growing rapport between them was that George wrote poems and showed them to Louisa for her approbation.

Louisa Powell was not considered a beauty by her family although she had a dainty well-proportioned figure. Her features were rather irregular but she had lovely eyes and her face was full of character. She was rather diffident and felt herself inferior in looks and charm to those of her sister-in-law Helen whom she knew George admired. But George did not judge by appearances. It was her personality he was in love with. She was vivacious with a great sense of humour and above all honest in her opinions. She hated hypocrisy and pretence and was discerning in detecting it. In her humility she felt herself

46

unworthy of George's attention as she knew she could not aspire to his great and transparent love for God.

It is not surprising that during his tutorship George spent as much time as possible at The Limes, much to the annoyance of the wife of his employer who being narrow-minded feared that the tutor she had employed for her sons was being led astray by the hot-headedness of youth. George must have disliked this intrusion into his private life as Hugh Sutherland had resented the laird's wife objecting to his visiting the Elginbrods and young Margaret, in particular. He resolved to terminate his appointment as soon as possible, but the necessity of earning sufficient money to pay off some college debts prevented him from acting hastily.

In the meantime, in between the tutoring and his visits to The Limes he continued to read widely, write poetry and develop his acquaintance with the Powells. Yet his overriding desire was still to find some means of preaching the Gospel, and for this reason he could not wholly relinquish the idea of training for the Ministry. He finally resigned his tutorship in the spring of 1848 and shortly after went north to visit his father and his home where he spent the summer of 1848. He had two important matters to discuss, one was the question of whether he should take a course at a theological College in preparation for the Congregational Ministry, in spite of his reservations with regard to dogma, and the other was his desired engagement to Louisa. He would take neither step without the approval of his father whose opinions he valued so highly. There in the familiarity of his childhood home he was able to relax briefly. He felt from his father's confidence in him and his sympathetic understanding of his difficulties that, with his advice, he would make the right decision. Though he respected his father's counsel MacDonald was by no means lacking in personal conviction; he had shed the Calvinism and dogmatic interpretation of the Gospel which he had been brought up on, for an infinitely freer and more direct approach in which his own conscience and experience played a paramount part.

In September 1848 he returned to London and enrolled as a student at Highbury Congregational College. It was one of five

Congregational Colleges in the London area. MacDonald chose Highbury because he had friends there. One of these, Robert Troup had already been a year at the college.

The academic standard of theological studies offered was high considering it was not the department of a University. Its three professors were distinguished each in his own field, Dr Ebenezer Henderson a great Hebrew scholar, Dr William Smith more widely known outside his own College for his *Latin Dictionary* and Professor John Godwin, a lecturer in Systematic Theology and a stimulating and radical teacher of New Testament exegesis. It was with John Godwin that George MacDonald felt most affinity. Not only was he to become related to him by marriage as Godwin married his wife's sister Charlotte, but George derived inspiration and confirmation of his own view from the professor's interpretation of the New Testament. Godwin tended to have a more liberal approach, amounting almost to Arminianism, the teaching of the Dutch reformed theologian who opposed Calvinism, in that he emphasised the importance of free-will and emphatically rejected the idea of predestination. Strangely enough, however, a few years later he took George to task for speaking his mind on such matters in his Church at Arundel and failing to tell the congregation in his sermons what they wanted to hear.

Living conditions at Highbury College were much more agreeable and conducive to study and serious thought than those in Fulham. Students had a bedroom and sitting-room each and good food was provided at the meals which they shared in common. Godwin was regarded as the principal and was resident in the college which gave George opportunities of getting to know him well. Apart from the academic work, there were extra curricula activities like debating and informal discussions on such subjects as the aesthetics of public worship and ghosts; on either of these topics George would not have been slow to express his opinions as he felt deeply about them. On the first he deplored the ugliness and lack of taste in non-conformist chapels, and with regard to the second, his firmly held Christian belief in the immortality of the soul made it difficult for him to rule out the possibility of the existence of ghosts, for 'the roots of the seen remain unseen' *(Castle Warlock)*.

The students met daily both morning and evening for bible reading and prayer. They also attended outside lectures at Marylebone Institute, where, for example, MacDonald heard A.J. Scott preach for the first time. This man to whom MacDonald dedicated one of his greatest novels *Robert Falconer*, later became Principal of Owens College, Manchester, and it was there that a firm friendship was established between them. Another friendship which developed during this period was with his fellow student James Matheson. The Mathesons lived in Islington only a few minutes walk from the College. Mrs Matheson a widow, kept open house for the Highbury students and it wasn't long before George was invited and introduced to James' brother Greville who became a life long friend, confidante and critic. The Mathesons were invited by the Powells to The Limes for charade parties which gave George further opportunities of getting to know them. All the Matheson children, six boys and one girl, were of exceptional intelligence. Although Congregationalists, they do not appear to have been so strict as the Powells and in the company of James and Greville, George occasionally attended the theatre. He also went to the National Gallery and Royal Academy and mentions admiring a picture by Turner, though unfortunately he forgot his glasses.

After he had been a month at Highbury and had begun to find his feet, he responded to his emotions and wrote to James Powell asking permission to broach the subject of marriage with Louisa. Although from a social and economic standpoint George had nothing to recommend him and his health was far from good, Powell gladly agreed. Over the past three years he had seen much of George and had come to recognize his true worth, his deep spirituality, sincerity and the charisma and charm of his personality. As Greville MacDonald affirms in the biography Louisa's mother loved him too.

There is no record of how the proposal was made, but Louisa accepted. The correspondence between them referring to this period speaks of the engagement as imminent and likely. George prays that divine love may make their love stronger, more real and more self-denying, but they can only expect to be a blessing to each other by doing right. Louisa writes with touching humility and reverence.

George MacDonald to Louisa Powell
Highway College
My Study Oct. 23rd 1848

I meant to write a much longer letter to my Louisa and many, beautiful and wise things (to me) I wanted to say, but now the impulse has left me. May our Father in Heaven be with you and bless you, and make you better of your present suffering.

Is love a beautiful thing dearest? You and I love: but who created love? Let us ask him to purify our love to make it stronger and more real and more self-denying. I want to love you for ever — so that, though there is not marrying or giving in marriage in heaven, we may see each other there as the best beloved. Oh Louisa, is it not true that our life here is a growing unto life, and our death a being born - our true birth? If there is anything beautiful in this our dreamy life, shall it not shine forth in glory in the bright awakening consciousness of heaven? And in our life together, my dear Louisa, if it please God that we should pass any part of our life together here, shall it not still shine when the cloud is over my head? I may see the light shining from your face, and when the darkness is around you, you may see the light on mine, and thus we shall take courage. But we can only expect to have this light within us and on our faces — we can only expect to be a blessing to each other — by doing that which is right....

Miss Louisa Powell to George MacDonald
Nov. 2nd 1850

You know how much and often I regret my want of the *enchanting* for your sake.., but indeed dearest believe me, in truth I say the better part of me would choose rather to be loved, as I believe you love me, than with the more *intoxicated admiration* — love that at first sight seems so enviable. What could I ask for more than the enduring affection I believe you have for me which you know is appreciated and treasured by me?...It is dear of you to say *we will love each other for ever* — it makes my heart happy every time you say so; for it is a strange one for fancying miseries and dreading the time when you will get tired of me, and I shall have no genius, no talent, no poetry, no beauty to win back the dear cherished love. My real hope is in growing better and in trusting that goodness may do what the others could not.

But enough of this. Your dear, dear letter requires no other answer than that I too love you more than ever — and that is saying a great deal. I feel so frightened sometimes putting such thoughts on paper, but no one knows but you — and you will not be shocked. The thought of our Heavenly Father knowing every word and seeing my thoughts does not distress me, but the opposite....

It was usual for students at Highbury to be sent out to various churches to undertake preaching engagements and to gain experience. They received payment for doing so which was an asset for George as he was most anxious that his father should not incur any debts on his behalf. In June 1849, six months after he had begun the course, MacDonald was sent to Cork in Ireland for three months. It was hard for the pair to be parted so soon after the engagement, but the separation had the effect of deepening their love for each other. Louisa wrote to him in a mystical vein;

Louisa Powell to George MacDonald at Cork
August 6th 1849

I had such a beautiful dream last night dear. I dreamt I had a vision, it was so beautiful! I think it was at sunset. I was looking earnestly at the clouds when one thick volume of pink and white cloud had two faces.... I looked at them for a long time not knowing who it was but soon discovered your face, only grown into a beautiful old man with the most glorified and perfectly beautiful expression upon it. The other for some time I thought was Mama, but upon looking and thinking I hoped it was I, with long white hair. I held a book out of which you were reading. You had your arm round my neck.... I dreamt that after looking for some time, the cloud melted away: then someone told me it was a vision sent to me that I might not fear present evil to either of us...

The separation was a test too for George with regard to his earnestness in desiring to enter the Ministry. It gave him confidence. His sermons seem to be well received and he himself felt satisfied at the way he was able to express his ideas.

Another month's preaching followed at Whitehaven and now, with the prospect of matrimony in view he began to consider what salary he might expect. He consulted his father on the subject but characteristically he replied that the work was more important than the stipend and that he should not think of marrying till his debt was paid off.

George MacDonald's brother Charles was by this time living in

Manchester where he had a good business appointment. He had recently married and had already attached himself to a fashionable Congregational Church as deacon. Manchester at this time was particularly prosperous owing to the boom in cotton. Charles was anxious for George to apply for a post as assistant minister at a fashionable church in the city which he believed would command a good stipend, but George turned it down, assuming it to be an example of Charles' wishful thinking.

MacDonald began to realize as he considered various possible pulpits that his unorthodox views were becoming more generally known and this would make him unacceptable in many churches. Considerably worried about this, George wrote to his father for advice. As always George MacDonald senior was the essence of common sense. He believed that extremes in matters of dogma tended to distort the truth whether it be selective salvation as in Calvinism or liberalism with its emphasis on free-will and free thought which glorified intellectualism, robs the Gospel of its mystery and turns the church into a debating society. George derived comfort from this letter as it showed that his father might be more flexible with regard to Calvinistic doctrines than he had imagined. At the same time he shrank from the idea of further discussion since he would feel obliged to express beliefs which to his father would seem heretical.

The year 1850 was a sad one for the Powell family. Mrs Powell died in September, and was sorely missed. The whole family went to Brighton for a change of air and scene. About that time MacDonald was offered a temporary pulpit at Arundel, twenty-five miles away. The comparatively short distance made it possible for the couple to meet more frequently, the Powells coming over to hear George preach and to criticise his reading of scripture and George spending any time available to him for recreation with the family at Brighton.

Arundel was a small country town on the banks of the river Arun, at the foot of Arundel Castle, the home of the Duke of Norfolk. The inhabitants were for the most part simple people, farmers or shopkeepers. They were friendly and gave the new minister a warm welcome. For a description of the town and some of the parishioners we can turn to *Annals of a Quiet Neighbourhood*. The village lay along one side of the river which was bordered by pollards; a lane led down to the river and through a meadow where brown and white cows grazed in the thick deep grass. Beyond the meadows were wooded slopes where fallow deer fed. Further along the river was the watermill and over its clear surface water beetles skimmed and 'one glorious dragonfly hovered making a mist about him with his long wings'. The river was navigable by fairly large vessels, bringing trade to the little town. A fine bridge spanned the Arun and it was here that MacDonald met one of the most endearing parishioners, Old Roger, who had served on a man o' war and used to good effect all the vocabulary associated with his calling. To Roger the pulpit was the mast-head, and he praised the parson for singing out 'Land ahead, or breakers ahead giving directions accordin'.

At first George MacDonald seems to have given satisfaction and after a month's temporary period of duty he received a call from the congregation to be the minister at a salary of £150 a year. George was not yet ordained, but he himself felt a call to be the equivalent of ordination and therefore a sufficient credential. But his father felt that as in George's case there was already to a certain extent some doubt as to the orthodoxy it would be best to comply with the desire of the congregation for his ordination.

In the meantime George threw himself whole heartedly into his preaching. Unfortunately the strain of adapting himself to his new duties as well as the damp and low-lying situation of Arundel took their toll and he succumbed to bronchitis followed by a severe haemorrhage of the lungs. He was living in lodgings at the time and Louisa was beside herself with anxiety when she heard of his illness. She wanted to go at once and nurse him, but propriety forbade it. She was reassured however on hearing from George himself that the landlady, Mrs New was kind and attentive and that the drastic and unpleasant treatment of leeches applied to his chest was doing him good.

Not only did the ordination have to be postponed, but George had to pay £2 a week to locums from his already inadequate salary. He spent his convalescence with an aunt in the Isle of Wight aided by a cure which was even less acceptable than the leeches — large quantities of cod liver oil, which he found difficult to keep down. Convalescence is often more trying than an actual illness and George found himself depressed and despondent and once again doubtful about his future. Like Mr Walton in *Annals of a Quiet Neighbourhood* grave doubts as to whether he was in his place in the church would keep rising and floating about like rain clouds within him. What were his motives? He did not know. Had he any right to be in the church eating her bread and drinking her wine without knowing whether he was fit to do her work? The only answer he could find was 'The Church is part of God's world. He makes men to work. Somehow or other I find myself in the Church and I see no other work to do. With God's help I will try to do it well. *(Annals of a Quiet Neighbourhood)*

George MacDonald wrote his dramatic poem, the first work to be published, called 'Within and Without' while convalescing, as its dedication to Louisa recalls:

Thou knowst its story, how for forty days
Weary with sickness and with social haze,
(After thy hands and lips with love divine
Had somewhat soothed me, made the glory shine
Though with a watery lustre) more delays
Of blessedness forbid — I took my ways
Into a solitude, Invention's mine.
There thought and wrote, afar, and yet with thee.

In January 1851 George returned to Arundel partially recovered yet still finding preaching a burden. His congregation seemed glad to see him. In the meantime preparations were going ahead for his wedding which had been fixed for Saturday, 8 March at the Old Gravel Pits Meeting House at Hackney, a chapel which the Powell family used to attend before they moved to Clapton Park. Before the wedding George stayed with his dear friends the Mathesons. He was very excited and had been busy with the joyful task of preparing a home for Louisa. He had rented a house in Tarrant Street in Arundel and had been making sure that the cooking arrangements were adequate, that there was proper accommodation for books and that the blinds were in working order. The guests and well-wishers were mainly members of the Powell family, but the Mathesons were there in full force. Characteristically on the very next day, Sunday, George preached at a church in Rugby, en route for his honeymoon at a relative's house in Leamington. The whole occasion went without a hitch, the only casualty being his Sunday trousers which in the packing were unfortunately baptised with the inevitable cod-liver oil!

George gave Louisa a unique wedding present, a beautiful poem in six stanzas which from a worldly standpoint could hardly be regarded as encouraging, but coming from the heart and pen of George MacDonald was poignant and strangely prophetic yet full of Christian hope:

Love me beloved for thou mayst be
Dead in my sight, neath the same blue sky.
Love me, O love me and let me know
The love that within thee moves to and fro
That many a form of thy love may be
Gathered around thy memory.

and it ended

'Pray God beloved for thee and me
That our souls may be wedded eternally'.

Life for the Minister was very different after his marriage. With a wife such as Louisa to care for his bodily needs, to see that he had food at regular times and to take an intelligent and sympathetic interest in his work, George's health improved and he was able to give himself more completely to his ministry. Louisa was popular with the parishioners and neighbours as she was very warm-hearted and took a genuine interest in their welfare. She was also practical and had a redeeming sense of humour which was a great help to her husband when he tended to take problems too seriously. They had a little garden where Louisa sowed flower seeds.

George loved the people and wanted them to be happy by living good lives. He preached a social gospel, trying to show them how they could apply Christ's standards in their daily work and in their homes. For this reason in his sermons he concentrated less on weighty matters of doctrine which he felt too often quenched the tender fires of the Holy Spirit, and tried to show how dishonesty and sharp practices in trade and in dealing with one's neighbours was incompatible with the Christian life. Like Thomas Wingfold, the curate in *Paul Faber*, MacDonald often preached on the text 'You cannot serve God and mammon'. The sermon Wingfold preached may actually be one of George's own. Many of the congregation were shop-keepers and they resented its implications, but he was a great friend of children and the poor.

In June that year George MacDonald was ordained. His friend and former Highbury teacher, John Godwin came for the occasion and also two of his brothers, Alec and John. It was then that Godwin met his future wife Charlotte Powell, Louisa's sister, for the first time and two years later they were married. Now that the MacDonalds had a home of their own they were kept busy with the visits of friends and relations, the Powells and the Mathesons. They had a visit too from George's brother John who was a school master and also wrote poetry, some of which was published with George's own verse together with some by his friend Greville Matheson in 'A Threefold Cord'.

For the remainder of the year George settled down to his ministry and began to find it rewarding. He was loved for his transparent goodness and genuine concern for the people's welfare and the few dissenting voices were not yet very loud. Although his health was still not very robust he was able to relax by writing poetry, and his greatest literary achievement of the period was the translation of *The Twelve Spiritual Songs* of Novalis which he circulated privately. Meanwhile George and Louisa awaited eagerly the birth of their first child. Lilia Scott MacDonald was born on 4th January, 1852 and was an immediate joy to her parents. She was the first of a succession of babies, eleven in all, the birth of each being welcomed as George MacDonald, senior, the proud grandfather put it, as 'one of the wonders of the world'.

George had a great affection for both John and his second youngest brother Alec. The three brothers had much in common. Each was in some measure kindled with the flame of enterprise and adventure. They had poetic imagination and religious fervour though it did not take the same form in each brother. Alec was more practical; John a philosopher, while George was a mystic. Alec was in business in Manchester and John a successful school master, but both died as young men in their twenties from the then universal scourge, tuberculosis.

The MacDonalds' married life which had begun so happily in Arundel was soon to be disrupted. A group of rich deacons in the Congregational Church who had taken umbrage at their minister's preaching, were resolved on getting their revenge by trying to force him to resign. One of them whose house the MacDonalds rented heard that George was looking for a larger one, which was reasonable owing to the increase in his family. The deacon chose to interpret this as a sign that the minister was receiving a larger salary than he needed and suggested to the congregation that his stipend of £150 should be reduced by £38. He hoped by this means to force his resignation. There is a pen portrait of this deacon in *David Elginbrod* in the pious but mean butcher Mr Appleditch whose odious little boy, Hugh Sutherland was forced to tutor for eighteen pence a day. George MacDonald himself actually taught the landlord deacon's son. He was as obnoxious and mercenary as his father and boasted like Appleditch's boy that he had five bags of gold in the Bank of England.

But George MacDonald was not to be so easily got rid of. Never in the whole course of his life did he allow his conduct to be influenced by financial considerations. He accepted the cut regretfully but he refused to resign unless he could be satisfied that this was the will of the whole congregation amongst whom he had many friends and well-wishers who showed their sympathy in a practical way, bringing produce from their garden or farm: fruit, vegetables or home-brewed beer.

Eventually however the deacons decided that if they could not dislodge their minister by financial means they must resort to theological ones. A certain section of the congregation had taken exception to George's preaching about the final destiny of unbelievers. He implied that their fate was not irrevocably determined on the day of their death but that they might yet obtain salvation after a sojourn in purgatory. Among other matters of seemingly minor importance perhaps, but about which George Mac-

Donald felt strongly, was the strictness of the Calvinistic Sabbath. He had suffered from it in Scotland and discovered that in England congregationalists were equally extreme. Another surprising objection came from a group of elderly ladies. The minister had been guilty of expressing a belief in the immortality of animals. As MacDonald saw it, they are part of the whole creation 'waiting for adoption' to quote St Paul and they have a right to considerate treatment from man. This theme is developed later on in 1878 in a sermon by Thomas Wingfold in *Paul Faber*. It is a passionate attack on vivisection and experiments on animals, a controversial subject even to-day. The text is 'are not two sparrows sold for a farthing and one of them shall not fall on the ground without your father'. This is obviously the voice of George MacDonald speaking

> 'It is true that we are above the creatures but not to keep them down, they are for our use and service but neither to be trodden under the foot of pride nor misused as ministers, at their worst cost of suffering, to our inordinate desires for ease. After no such fashion did he give them to be our helpers in living. To be tortured that we might gather ease — none but a devil could have made them for that. When I see a man who professes to believe not only in a God but such a God as holds his court in the person of Jesus Christ, assail with miserable cruelty the scanty lovely timorous lives of the helpless about him, it sets my soul aflame with such indignant wrath…that I have to make haste and rush to the feet of the master'.

The deacons had got wind also of the fact that he had sent copies of his translation of the *Sacred Songs of Novalis* to certain of his friends the previous Christmas, and they used the knowledge to accuse him of entertaining heretical views based on German Theology. George MacDonald's Christmas message to his friends from Novalis was not one they wished to hear.

> Uplifted is the stone
> And all mankind arisen!
> We are thy very own,
> We are no more in prison!
> What bitterest grief can stay
> Beside thy golden cup,
> When earth and life give way
> And with our Lord we sup!

Lost, lost are all our losses!
Love is for ever free!
The full life heaves and tosses
Like an unbounded sea!
One live, eternal story!
One poem high and broad!
And sun of all our glory
The countenance of God!'

At a meeting held on July 5th 1852, MacDonald as their pastor, addressed the congregation saying that as he came in the first place at the invitation of the whole church, it would be unfair to other members to resign unconditionally on account of the dissatisfaction of the few. About twenty people were in agreement with the protest, but there is no record of the total membership of the Church at that time. George did not consider that a sufficient number were in favour of his resignation so he did nothing further about it for a time and continued to express in his sermons his own views on the subjects which had caused offence. But eventually a year later in May 1853, when he saw that his presence was causing a division in the congregation, he resigned.

The MacDonalds stayed on in their house in Arundel for a time. In July George went up to London to marry his friend the Revd J.H. Godwin to his sister-in-law Charlotte. A slight coolness had arisen between the former teacher and his pupil. Godwin was disappointed with George's failure to win the approval of the Arundel congregation, although he himself held many of the liberal views which had caused George's downfall. He seemed to imply that a new minister should try to accommodate his own beliefs to those held by his people. Though surprised at Godwin's viewpoint, George did not allow the matter to come between them.

On July 23rd, 1853 the MacDonalds' second child, Mary Josephine was born.

Manchester

George MacDonald's first venture into professional life could not be called successful, yet it was far from being a total failure. His experience as Minister of Arundel Congregational Church had made it clear to him that he must not answer another call from a congregation as a result of which he would be expected to tow the orthodox line on Calvinist doctrine in opposition to the dictates of his conscience. The problem for him now was to find an alternative way to earn his living which would be compatible with his evangelistic ideals, and at the same time enable him to provide for his wife and two children.

The immediate solution was for the family to stay temporarily at The Limes where they would be welcomed by Louisa's father and the sisters who were still living at home. MacDonald himself did not wish to burden the Powells with his presence too. He must have felt a little sensitive in failing to support his family after so short a time, and he probably thought it would be better to try to make a fresh start in new surroundings. Being a Scot in exile, he had not much acquaintance with other parts of England so he naturally felt drawn to Manchester where his brother Charles already lived with his new wife and recent business appointment.

More importantly, Professor A.J. Scott lived there, whom MacDonald had greatly admired when he was at University College, London, both for his religious views and as a man. Scott was a universalist and had in his younger days in Paisley been found guilty of heresy by the presbytery and forbidden to preach. George MacDonald regarded him as the greatest intellect he had known and he later dedicated his book *Robert Falconer* to Scott as the man 'who stands highest in the oratory of my memory'. A.J. Scott was by now the Principal of Owens College, Manchester where he held the Chair of Mental Philosophy and English Literature. He welcomed George MacDonald, and throughout his stay in Manchester did all he could to relieve his poverty and to further MacDonald's ambitions to find opportunities for preaching and teaching, qualities for which Scott had a great respect.

Geographically and meteorologically no place could have been a greater contrast to Arundel than Manchester with its fog-bound air and grimey streets filled with pale-faced workers trying to earn a living in the cotton mills. Hardly the place for one who even in the pure air of Arundel had suffered perpetually from bronchitis. George recorded his impressions of the city in 'A Midsummer Poem':

Tis a poor drizzly morning, dark and sad.
The cloud has fallen, and filled with fold on fold
The chimneyed city; and the smoke is caught,
And spreads diluted in the cloud, and sinks,
A black precipitate, on miry streets.
And faces gray glide through the darkened fog....
In labour they pass the murky day,
'Mid floating dust of swift-revolving wheels,
And filmy spoil of quick contorted threads,
Which weave a sultry chaos all about;
Until at length, old darkness, swelling slow
Up from the caves of night to make an end,
Chokes in its tide the clanking of the looms,
The monster engines, and the flying gear....

To one who lives in these surroundings George MacDonald concludes

And the first daisy on a wind-swept lea
[is] Dearer than Eden-groves with rivers four.

He was appalled at the depths of poverty which he found – conditions being worse even than those he had come across in Aberdeen.

He arrived in Manchester in July 1853 and remained there for two and a half years. It was a time of disappointment and great privation. To begin with he had no work to do, nowhere to live and his health was unreliable.

But he was not down-hearted; he continued to pursue any opportunities which presented themselves. He stayed for a time with his brother Charles in Radnor Street and meanwhile applied for the post of librarian at Owens College which unfortunately he did not get. His main concern was to raise a congregation on whom he could practise his considerable powers as a preacher.

In September he mentioned in a letter to his father that a group of personal friends and acquaintances were anxious for him to preach if a room could be found but there would probably be no remuneration. It was by now clear to many people that MacDonald was an eloquent preacher with undoubted charisma. An old woman in one of his congregations later said to MacDonald senior, 'when I saw him wi' the moustaches I thocht it was like Christ himsel speakin' to me'. He could have been much in demand in a fashionable Church and commanded a large stipend had he been prepared to compromise his conscience and give the congregation what they wished to hear, but he was not prepared to do this.

The family did not come together again till February 1854 when the MacDonalds moved to lodgings in Manchester. Louisa and the children had in the meantime been staying with her brother's family in Liverpool. George joined them for Christmas but Louisa found it went against the grain to be constantly accepting charity from friends and relations. Although MacDonald had great sympathy with his wife's point of view, it did not seem to bother him. He humbly accepted hospitality from whatever source. At one time he was entertained during a preaching engagement in Birkenhead by a rich businessman with a carriage for his own use. At another the family found themselves in an old farmhouse with stone walls and low open-beamed ceilings − at Alderly in Cheshire, put at their disposal by a sister of A.J. Scott. Fortunately Louisa was a wonderful manager and made a weekly income of ten shillings go further than anyone else. She was the kind of person who thrived on adversity. She had an adventurous spirit, a great sense of humour and a warm heart and she was soon accepted by the Manchester women in the neighbourhood whom she found friendly and without pretentions in spite of the fact that many of them were quite well to-do with husbands involved in commerce.

At last, in May, the MacDonalds were able to move into a house, Number Three, Camp Terrace in Lower Broughton at an annual rent of thirty-five pounds. The house provided a base from which other enterprises could be tried. They took a lodger Arthur Morley Francis, a former Highbury student and Louisa was able to take a few pupils. In the meantime George had obtained the post of journalist with *The Christian Spectator* and was doing a little coaching in English and Physical Science during the vacation; but the important development in June of that year was the provision of a room in Renshaw Street by a group of his followers where he could preach without any restrictions. There were no pew rents and so George had to rely on the charity of the congregation.

The tide was beginning to turn for him. At last he felt more settled and hopeful about his evangelistic aims and decided to refuse an invitation to join him from his uncle, MacIntosh Mackay, who had recently emigrated with some Highlanders. Louisa was a bad sailor and in any case it would have been inopportune as their third daughter Caroline Grace was born on September 16, 1854.

MacDonald was in constant communication with his home in Huntly. His letters cover a wide range of subjects; at one time he is describing his latest literary efforts or giving a progress report on his Sunday Services in Renshaw Street, at another requesting half a pound of fresh butter, or informing his father that he is growing a beard. He had tried the experiment earlier after he was engaged but had had to shave it off as his prospective father-in-law objected.

The academic side of his work was progressing. He was one of the original lecturers of Manchester Ladies College where he taught English, Natural Philosophy and later on Mathematics. In his spare time between teaching and preaching, George had been putting the finishing touches to the dramatic poem he had begun at Arundel, 'Within and Without' for which he hoped to find a publisher. While on a visit to London staying at The Limes, he read it aloud to the Powell family and his friend Greville Matheson. An interesting event which he attended during the same visit was F.D. Maurice's inaugural address to the Working Men's College recently established. This was George's introduction to a man who was to become one of his greatest friends.

1855 began auspiciously for George MacDonald with the acceptance for publication of his manuscript of *Within and Without*. He wrote off to his father the very next day to tell him the good news. George had long been hoping to visit his family in Huntly but lack of funds prevented it. Now he hoped to be able to afford it. There was a special reason for desiring to make the journey as soon as possible as his little twelve year old step-sister Bella with whom he often corresponded, was now incurably ill with tuberculosis and time was running out. A close bond existed between them, and they sometimes exchanged gifts. When Bella was twelve she sent her step-brother a knitted silk purse. In a letter of thanks he expressed in lyrical terms his love of his Huntly home and longing to be there again.

> How much I should like to spend a winter at home again, a snowy winter with great heaps and wreaths of snow: and sometimes the wild wind howling in the chimneys and against the windows and down at the kitchen door! And how much I should love to spend one long summer day in June lying on the grass before the house, and looking up into the deep sky with large white clouds in it. And when I lifted my head I should see the dear old hills all round about, and the shining of the Bogie whose rush I should hear far off and soft, making a noise hardly louder than a lot of midges.... And then the warmer evening, with long grass in the field where the well is, and the corn-craik crying craik-craik — somewhere in it though nobody knows where...

He had hoped that she would have been able to stay with them and attend the Ladies College. There was a further reason for going to Huntly. His cousin Margaret was engaged to Robert Troup his old Highbury friend and they had asked George to marry them.

In May 1855 *Within and Without* was published and was enthusiastically received. It put George MacDonald on the literary map as it were and through it he made useful contacts with several influential and distinguished people: Lady Byron for example, Charles Kingsley, John Ruskin and F.D. Maurice. The book was acclaimed on literary grounds as well as for its content: *The Scotsman* reported it to be 'full of the most exquisite poetry sustained at the pitch of sublimity with immense yet apparently effortless power'. Yet in the subject matter consists its raison d'être. The poem traces in dramatic form the history of a monk, Julian, who having tried in vain to find God in the abstractions and aspirations and arid routine of the monastic life escapes from the monastery and finds once again the girl he used to love. He rescues her from danger and they elope to England, but in spite of their mutual love for each other and for their child Lilia, they are not happy, the girl being unable to understand Julian's absorption with God. They drift apart and a rival for Lilia's affection appears in the shape of an Englishman. Julian is jealous and suspicious but eventually realises he is wrong to neglect Lilia and that she deserves his total love and that only by loving others unselfishly can we truly love God. He finds like Milton, that he cannot praise a fugitive and cloistered virtue. He must

> Go forth into the tumult and the shout,
> Work, love with workers, lovers, all about;
> Of noise alone is born the inward sense
> Of silence and from action springs alone
> The inward knowledge of true love and faith.

George MacDonald wrote the first draft of this poem during a period of convalescence at Arundel before his marriage. It is evidence of the conflict in his mind at that time between his love of God and desire to dedicate himself whole-heartedly to His service and his natural physical love for Louisa. In the poem the struggle is resolved and George in the character of Julian wins through to the realisation that spiritual and earthly love are not incompatible as long as there is no selfishness in the human love. They are but reverse sides of the same coin. George wrote the poem not only to reassure himself that his love for Louisa was good and holy, but, also, to convince her that he truly loved her and that he returned the love she evidently felt for him. He dedicated it to her.

> Receive thine own for I and it are thine

But George MacDonald could not waste time savouring his victory and waiting for the reviews to pour in. The news from Huntly regarding Bella was bad, and having now the means to travel, with Louisa's encouragement he set off for Scotland. He broke his journey in Edinburgh and was appalled at the filth and squalor of the Grassmarket, and the Canongate, the worst slums he had seen so far. But soon all was forgotten as he found himself once again in the familiar surroundings of his childhood home. He took up the old life where he had left it off, riding over the countryside on the dear white mare Missy, climbing the one thousand feet of Clashmach hill two and a half miles from his home, and taking leisurely walks by the river and up to the Castle. He was anxious to preach in the Church of his youth. His Uncle James was an Elder there and was rather suspicious of his nephew's unorthodox views, but he eventually withdrew his opposition and George was invited.

But always there was the knowledge that little Bella was 'wearing awa' to the land of the leal'. He spent much time with her and sent away for a book of *Grimms' Fairy Tales* to give her.

MacDonald still valued the talks he was able to have with his father. They both enjoyed and discussed the poems of Robert Browning, and George was delighted that his father seemed to have accepted his beard and even said he had no objection to him growing it till he had to stuff it into his trousers!

Meanwhile poor Louisa was trying to cope on her own with the trials of domestic life. When George was with her his philosophical attitude carried her through, but without him, even minor crises looked like major catastrophies. They had both hoped that she and the children would have been able to accompany him to Scotland, but unfortunately funds would not allow it. In her regular letters to her husband we read of her desperate attempts to raise enough for the fare by painting a chess table on slate for her brother for which she was to receive £6, quite a large sum in those days, but time and energy were in short supply and the table made little progress. Added to this her nursemaid Charlotte was 'playing up' in George's absence. She was rude to her mistress and ended up by breaking the perambulator and the children were ailing for lack of fresh air. The new one cost 24 shillings and proved too heavy for Louisa to push. In addition the grocer required settlement of his account. Louisa was forced to borrow from her family which made her feel very inferior.

Up in Scotland, George had at the time of receiving these tales of woe from his wife only 2/6 in his pocket, but it did not seem to worry him.

Letter to Louisa August 1st 1855

I have just 2/6. I spend nothing here. I had 4s when I arrived and I have spent a shilling for stamps which I need not do except I liked but one doesn't like to be going to the office for stamps always.

My father has just come in and offered me £3 to send to you. I have not taken it yet for I dare say you will not want any before you can answer this and tell me how much you will need till I see you again.

He was soon home again with a reliable Scottish maid Elsie from Huntly who helped to restore order and contentment in the Manchester home, and all for the modest wage of £7 a year.

A letter to Louisa from her husband in July of that year shows some slight indication that George realised what it meant to Lousia to be married to a mystic:

I know what my wife is worth. You have a harder trial than others dear, both from your husband being what he is and poor besides — but perhaps that may be made up to you some day.

Joseph Johnson in his biography of George MacDonald calls him a *mystic* on the grounds that in him, 'spiritual apprehensions of truth often transcend his appreciations of mundane necessities.' Louisa would surely have agreed.

In August Bella died making a second gap in the family circle following so closely after his brother Alec's death. George wrote comfortingly to his step-mother, his words illumined by faith in the after life:

Dear Mother, who could wish an easier, quieter, simpler death than my dear sister's? I should like to wither away out of the world like the flowers that they may come again....

and that as it happened was exactly what George MacDonald himself was to do sixty years later. George's words to his step-mother find an echo in David Elginbrod's prayer on learning of the death of Hugh Sutherland's father. 'O Thou in whose sicht oor deith is precious, an' no licht maitter; wha through darkness leads to licht, an' through deith to the greater life! — we canna' believe that thou wouldst gie us any guid thing, to tak' the same again; for that would be but bairns' play....'

Back in Manchester MacDonald was busy developing the scope of his preaching commitments. While at Renshaw Street his congregation consisted mainly of middle class intellectuals, in Bolton he was ministering to the working class; spinners, weavers and mechanics who were living well below the poverty line in shameful conditions. They worked unreasonably long hours and George had great sympathy with their plight. It gave him pleasure to help them, but unfortunately in November he became ill again from another haemorrhage of the lungs. His sister-in-law, Angela Powell came to help nurse him, the Scotts were very attentive and his father-in-law paid the rent of the house in Camp Terrace, while donations flowed in from various well-wishers, so that his convalescence was not hindered by financial worry.

In January 1856 the MacDonalds first-born son arrived and was called Greville after George's great friend Greville Matheson. After this joyous event George went to convalesce for a while with his friends the Scotts. By this time he was feeling rather depressed as he realised that he was not strong enough to continue his preaching commitments just when the congregation was beginning to become established. It was becoming clear to him and to the family that Manchester with its smoke and perpetual damp was not the climate for one with chronic bronchial trouble. In February therefore they let the house in Camp Terrace and moved down first to London for the wedding of Louisa's sister Phoebe and then to furnished accommodation at Kingswear in Devon where unfortunately MacDonald again had a recurrence of his bronchial trouble. The Vicar, the Revd John Smart and his wife showed great kindness and concern and subsequently became life-long friends. The MacDonalds eventually moved to Lynmouth to complete George's convalescence. They spent three months there and the whole family, the four children by this time being four, three, two and four months respectively, grew fat on eggs and Devonshire cream. They were at an enchanting age. Greville MacDonald records his father's memory of them in the biography 'the little white Lily with her wondering grey eyes, her sensitive nostrils, her rare sweet smile and that captivating quick-blossoming of her roses; the little dark-haired elfish Mary with her blackbird's voice and a sweetness more instant than Lily's; the solemn less pretty Gracie but with her mother's wonderful eyes, and the great greedy baby, his brown eyes all for his mother'.

But in spite of the health-giving West Country air MacDonald had not yet fully recovered his strength, so at the suggestion of Lady Byron, one of his admirers and friends by correspondence, George, Louisa and the second child little Mary, set out to winter in the warmth of Algiers at her expense. The long suffering Louisa was loth to go, partly because of dreaded sea-sickness and also because she hated the idea of being separated from her other children who were left in the care of her sister. But when she saw how delighted her husband was with everything he saw, she unselfishly overcame her reluctance. George wrote ecstatically to his father of the blue of the Mediterranean, bluer than other seas, of the orange trees outside their hotel window and the colourful costumes of the cosmopolitan population, Arabs, Jews and Moors as well as Turks and Armenians mounted on mules and donkeys. Later they moved to an old house on a hillside surrounded by olive groves which although inclined to be damp afforded splendid views of the Mediterranean, its blue-green waters streaked with purple. Westward in the far distance towered the snow-capped peaks of the Atlas mountains. In Algiers they made the acquaintance of some interesting people − the Leigh-Smiths, cousins of Florence Nightingale and Mrs Oliphant the novelist whose father was a publisher in Edinburgh.

In the words of Mrs Ormonde (daughter of William Oliphant an Edinburgh publisher), who met George MacDonald at this time, 'in Algiers he seemed as happy as a schoolboy'. His capacity for enjoyment was very noticable. This bright joyousness characterised all his writing. It was a product of his child-like faith in God's goodness.

The visit was marred only by the fact that little Mary contracted opthalmia and was totally blind for a time, but MacDonald returned in April 1857 with a volume of poetry ready for publication. This included his poignantly beautiful saga of a young crofter, *A Hidden Life*. In the farmer's son George sees his brother Alec, who died as a young man of tuberculosis debilitated by grief at the loss of the girl he loved. Alec's engagement to a Sunday school teacher was broken off at the instigation of her parents when he developed serious lung disease. It could have applied in retrospect too to his brother John soon to follow Alec from the same disease and these words could be taken as referring to the death of both:

> In the hush of noon he died.
> The sun shone on − why should he not shine on?
> Glad summer noises rose from all the land;
> The love of God lay warm on hill and plain,
> Tis well to die in summer.
> ...when the breath
> After a hopeless pause, returned no more
> The father fell upon his knees and said
> 'O God I thank Thee it is over now!
> Through the sore time Thy hand has led him well
> Lord let me follow soon and be at rest.

Was this prophetic? A few days after John's death George MacDonald's father died of a heart attack. But not before his son George had visited him for the last time in July, a month after the publication of his poems. He felt bereft and realized how much he had relied on his father's wise advice and unfailing interest in his welfare. He was very concerned for his widowed step-mother and offered her and her two children a home with them. He returned in time for the birth of a fourth daughter, Irene on August 31st.

Since their return from Algiers the MacDonalds had been staying at The Limes, while George wound up his various commitments in Manchester having regretfully acknowledged at last that the climate was not for him. Now however it was important for a house to be found where they could all be together. With financial help from Lady Byron they finally rented a house in Hastings. It was on the Tackelway and was called Providence House, a suitable enough name for the domicile of such a family, but George and Louisa thought it too pretentious in spite of the fact that it had thirteen rooms, and they re-named it Huntly Cottage. It was a rambling old

71

building in a once fashionable area of the town, so the rent was only £35 a year. George hoped to be able to use one of the larger rooms for lectures. The house was built on a hillside and commanded magnificent views of the rooftops and church towers of the town, and beyond them of the sea. But above all it was home for the growing family.

It was October when they moved in and by Christmas, in spite of one or two bouts of bronchitis for MacDonald, they were settled in and what a Christmas it was and in keeping with the warmth and generosity of George and Louisa.

Greville records Louisa's diary account of it. 'How happy everyone looked! The big ones, none of them thinking of themselves, but all pleasing the little ones; and thus came their own pleasure'. Lady Byron had sent £50 and there were parcels and a bran cake from The Limes, but most of the festivities were provided for out of George's meagre resources. The nursery walls were adorned with seasonal pictures, such as robins, snow scenes and Christmas bells. There was a Christmas tree decorated with candles and hung with little presents, penny toys and books or gloves and handkerchiefs. Louisa was the life and soul of the occasion making caps and dresses for all the children as well as the big plum pudding, the last fittingly celebrated with capital letters in Louisa's diary. On the day itself, thirteen poor children were invited in to see the tree and receive presents. Afterwards each child was given a cake or bun and George told them the story of Christmas. Finally they went home, happy with half an orange each. It does not sound much perhaps by modern standards, but the MacDonalds gave out of their penury and what was given with so much love and without any feeling of condescension was no doubt gratefully received. Little Mary, or Elfie as they called her because she was small and delicate, was the only child there who could not enjoy the festival to the full as she was still suffering from opthalmia and could only feel her presents.

During this period the family settled into a routine. The children seem to have been well behaved though delicate and needing special care, but they were amenable to discipline and responded to their parent's care. Although the children gave the minimum of trouble they had an anxious time when George's brother John came to stay in April 1858. He was seriously ill with tuberculosis and in need of nursing, and at the same time was longing to go home to Huntly. He managed to do this in July but died a few days later at the age of twenty-eight. George was grief-stricken. He had always felt responsible for his brother.

Since before Christmas MacDonald had been working on a faerie romance called *Phantastes*. It took him only two months to complete and in January through his friend, F.D. Maurice, he found a publisher, Smith Elder. It was published in October 1858 only two months after the death of MacDonald's father. It must have grieved him that this book which was to be highly acclaimed in literary circles and contained the essence of his imaginative genius was destined never to gain the stamp of parental approval.

Of all George MacDonald's voluminous writings *Phantastes* has lived the longest in the world of literature and has had the greatest influence on other writers. It is an unusual book, traditional in that it echoes chivalrous romances such as Malory's *Morte d'Arthur* or Spenser's *Faerie Queen*, and yet unique in that it has another dimension; it contains an evocation of holiness and other-worldliness.

MacDonald probably derived the name *Phantastes* meaning 'imagination', from Phineas Fletcher's 'Purple Land', where Phantastes is described as one of the three councillors of the Castle of the Mind together with Judgement and Memory. To George MacDonald, imagination is the most powerful faculty of the human mind because by it the truth may be perceived and acted upon. It is the gateway to reality because it deals not with a fictional world apart from the pleasures and trials of daily life, but gives a deeper insight into their meaning and ultimate purpose.

The book relates the adventures of Anodos. These represent the experience of his own imagination which runs parallel with his natural physical life. The story traces the gradual purification of his imaginative powers as he faces temptation and accepts the challenge of danger and materialism. When he gives in to sensuality and sin he experiences remorse which dogs his footsteps like a dark shadow getting between him and the sun. It warps his vision and makes him unable to see other people as they really are, for the shadow is in his heart as well as at his heels. After many adventures and after he has humbly faced himself and his own failure and accepted the opportunity of making the supreme sacrifice by attacking a monster who is harming a knight and his lady, he experiences release from his shadow, knows the joy of conquering self and the blessedness of death which he discovers to be life itself. In the end he returns to a normal state of life with his imagination purged by the knowledge that all experiences work together for good and that for him evil is only the reverse side of the coin of good. He had learnt that in the country of Faerie which is the true world, a man may often fail in an individual act, for renown and success are of no great value but 'if he goes once again to work with a cool brain and strong will...the result of his life-time will content him'. As a result of his experience Anodos realised that 'art rescues nature from the weary and sated regards of our senses, and the degrading injustice of our anxious everyday life, and, appealing to the imagination, which dwells apart, reveals Nature in some degree as she really is, and as she represents herself to the eye of the child whose everyday life, fearless and unambitious meets the true import of the wonder-teeming world around him, and rejoices therein without questioning'.

It was this transfiguring of the actual world of everyday living which appealed to C.S. Lewis. In his preface to a modern edition of *Phantastes* Lewis describes the effect upon him of first reading the book when he found it on a station bookstall. He was already familiar with the romances of Malory, Spenser and Morris with their splendid tales of heroic deeds of chivalry , but *Phantastes* while dealing with equally romantic situations with fair maidens and grizzly monsters gave him something different. He did not feel remote from such adventures but felt himself to be concerned in them as part of his own experience. He identified himself with Anodos and knew the joy to be found in the realization of holiness in the common things of life. He had emerged from the dark shadow and found himself bathed in light. It was a baptism of his imagination. It was not an escape but

1. The house in Duke Street, Huntly, where George MacDonald was born.
Courtesy of North East of Scotland Library Service.

2. George MacDonald's second home 'The Farm', to which he moved while still a boy.
Courtesy of North East of Scotland Library Service.

3. 'The Square', Huntly, birthtown of George MacDonald.
   Courtesy of North East of Scotland Library Service.

4. 'The Retreat', Hammersmith, the house to which George MacDonald moved in 1867.
   Courtesy of Hammersmith Central Library.

5. Irene and Grace MacDonald in a pose
   inspired by Burne-Jones. Porto Fino
   1878 or 1879.
   Courtesy of MacDonald-Troup Collection.

6. 'Elsie sings Ranald asleep', illustration
   by Arthur Hughes from
   Ranald Bannerman's Boyhood,
   (Blackie and Son 1900 p.152)

7. George MacDonald with his daughter Lily by Lewis Carroll.
   Courtesy of The Gernsheim Collection – University of Texas.

8. Efford Cottage, Bude in Cornwall where George took his family for a holiday in 1867. *Courtesy of Rennie Bere.*

9. 'Casa Coraggio', Bordighera in Italy, a house planned and built by George MacDonald where he moved with his family in 1880. *Courtesy of Hammersmith Central Library.*

10. Louisa MacDonald and daughters, left to right, Irene, Lilia, Grace, Winifred, Louisa, 1878 or 1879.
Courtesy of MacDonald-Troup Collection.

11. George MacDonald and sons, left to right, Bernard Powell, Robert Faulkner, Greville Matheson, George, Ranald, Maurice, George Mackay, 1878 or 1879
Courtesy of MacDonald-Troup Collection.

12. George MacDonald, 1872 or 1873.
Courtesy of MacDonald-Troup Collection.

13. Louisa MacDonald, 1872 or 1873.
Courtesy of MacDonald-Troup Collection.

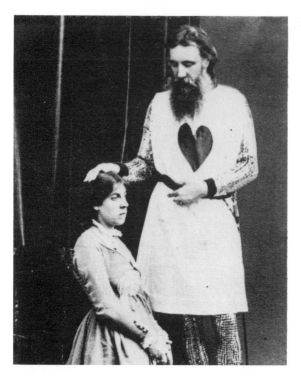

14. George MacDonald
    as Mr Greatheart with
    his daughter Grace as
    Mercy.
    *Courtesy of MacDonald-
    Troup Collection.*

15. The MacDonald Family at Bournemouth 1876 or 7. Left to right: standing; Greville,
    Grace, Ted Hughes (a friend), Ranald, Winifred. Seated: Maurice, Lilia, Louisa,
    George, Robert Faulkner?, Mary. On the ground: Bernard Powell?, Mary,
    George Mackay? *Courtesy of MacDonald-Troup Collection.*

an involvement. Henceforth romanticism became the vehicle for some of C.S. Lewis' most important and popular writing. He constructed a brave new world not as Aldous Huxley had done, foretelling a future state dehumanized by scientific progress but a milieu of primaeval innocence as of the morning of the world where goodness reigns and evil has no substance. Out of the land of Faerie, Lewis created the kingdom of Narnia, but not until a few years later when his imagination had been 'Christianized'.

In *The Great Divorce*, Lewis portrays himself as accompanying a party of lost souls in Hell on an excursion to Paradise. The theme has echoes of Dante's *Purgatorio*. With George MacDonald whom he meets there as his guide, Lewis discovers the weaknesses of character which prevent all but one in the expedition from wishing to remain there. *The Great Divorce* is an imaginative attempt to answer the questions 'What is purgatory like?' and 'Is it a permanent state?'

Phantastes abounds in some superbly romantic descriptions. Anodos falls into a trace of still delight when the beech tree wraps his arms around him. This is how he describes it:

'The rain in the leaves and a light wind that had arisen kept her song company. It told of the secret of the woods and the flowers and the birds. At one time I felt as if I was wandering in childhood through a sunny spring forest over carpets of primroses, anemonies and little white starry things. At another I lay dreaming in the hot summer noon with a book of old tales beside me.... in autumn I grew sad because I trod on leaves that had sheltered me and received their last blessing in the sweet odours of decay or in a winter evening frozen still looked up as I went home to a warm fireside through the nelled boughs and twigs to the cold snowy moon, with her opal zone around her'.

The description of the dragon is truly ghastly: 'The horrid serpent-like head with its black tongue forked with red hanging out of its jaws, dangled against the horse's side. Its neck was covered with long blue hair, its sides with scales of green and gold. Its back was of corrugated skin of a purple hue. Its belly was similar in nature but its colour was leaden dashed with blotches of livid blue' — a truly Spenserian monster. But it was not for these purple patches that Lewis valued *Phantastes* in his autobiography *Surprised by Joy* but rather for the 'bright shadow of holiness' which lay upon the land of Faerie and led Anodos to a happy grave. In his death Lewis himself found peace and his imagination lived again reborn. Anodos lay in his coffin with his hands folded in peace. The knight and the lady wept over him: 'He has died well' she said. The hot fever of life had gone and he breathed the bright mountain air of the land of Death.

Understandably therefore on his fictional excursion into Heaven in *The Great Divorce*, Lewis accepts George MacDonald as his guide and greets him as his master with an acknowledgement of his great indebtedness to *Phantastes* as the beginning of a new life, first in the realm of his imagination and eventually in his acceptance of Christianity and faith in life beyond the grave. It is not until he has accepted the Christian faith as credible that his non-academic writing blossoms and the flower is clearly influenced by his study of George MacDonald's writings. His wide knowledge of the master's work is demonstrated in the selection of passages from his sermons, faery romances and domestic novels which he published. The writing of both master and pupil is didactic, but the message in each case is one not of teaching but of discovery — the revelation of real life emanating, as in *Phantastes* for example, from such mundane things as the washstand in Anodos' bedroom out of which gushed a stream of living water or the wardrobe, the back of which Lucy discovered opened onto the Kingdom of Narnia.

London

MacDonald's writing inevitably progressed slowly and did not make him financially viable with a wife and six children to maintain; this was due to his indifferent health and uncertain lecturing commitments. Fortunately his reputation as a lecturer was growing and it was along these lines that he now looked to develop his career.

The break came in the summer of 1859 when he was asked to give four lectures at the London Institute, and engagements soon followed in Edinburgh and Manchester. His lecturing put him in touch with a wider literary circle and influential people in other walks of life. Foremost among these was Lady Byron an heiress, Anne Isabella Milbanke, who had married the poet in 1815 but left him the following year after the birth of their daughter Ada. By the time MacDonald met her in 1857 she was sixty five years old, living in London and devoting her still considerable wealth to philanthropic ends. She was a great admirer of MacDonald's writing and of *Within and Without* in particular. In gratitude to her for financing his Algiers visit, MacDonald sent her the following poem:

To A.L.N.B.

They followed hard for riches' sake,
The searching men of old
After the secret that would make
The meaner metals gold.
A nobler alchemy is thine,
O lady born to bless:
Gold in thy hand becomes divine —
Grows truth and tenderness.

Lady Byron was untiring in introducing him to people who she thought would be able to help him — Russell Gurney, the Recorder of London, and through him to John Ruskin. He was acquainted also with Charles Kingsley, Matthew Arnold and Lewis Carroll whom he had already met at Hastings. His friendship with Lady Byron had developed rapidly, the initiative coming from the lady herself. She was a most determined person but also extremely kind and generous. George MacDonald gives us a vivid portrait of her as Lady Bernard in *The Vicar's Daughter*. 'She was like a fountain of living water that could find no vent but into the lives of her fellows – Never did woman of rank step more triumphantly over the barriers... between the classes of society'. She set about persuading MacDonald that he would be much better off living in London, both from the point of view of health as well as being more likely to find openings for his academic career. The move was made in October 1859.

After renting a house in Queen's Square for six months, the MacDonalds moved into Tudor Lodge, Albert Street, Regents Park, an attractive red brick house with stone mullioned windows and a good sized garden where the children could play. Its attraction as far as George was concerned was a large studio which could serve as a lecture room. But it was not only for solemn occasions. Children's parties were held there too with George attired in a fur rug pretending to be a bear! Arthur Hughes, a newly made friend who later illustrated some of MacDonald's books, joined in charades with great enthusiasm.

About this time MacDonald was fortunate in obtaining the post of Professor of English Literature at Bedford College, London, founded by Mrs Read in 1849 as the first College to cater for women. The appointment gave him a stable, though small income. He continued there until 1867 and was delighted that his step-sister, Louie was able to become a student there and live with the family. But disappointment was again in store for him as a play which he had written was refused by a succession of publishers; added to which in May 1860 his good friend Lady Byron died, and shortly after in October there was another mouth to feed on the arrival of the second son, Ronald. Funds were at a low ebb and even the eldest child Lily was aware of the scarcity of food and pretended not to be hungry. George and Louisa prayed, affirming their trust in God and received it seemed an immediate answer — a letter from Lady Byron's executors containing a legacy of three hundred pounds.

Except for *The Portent,* a short story concerned with Celtic powers of second sight, which appeared in serial form in the Cornhill Magazine in 1860 nothing of George MacDonald's was published for five years after the appearance of *Phantastes,* but through George Murray Smith, the discerning head of the publishers, Smith Elder & Co. who held business dinners, George now made the acquaintance of literary giants such as Thackeray, Leslie Stephen and Leigh Hunt. But he was far from being an intellectual snob, and really preferred the company of simple undistinguished men. For there was a fundamental difference in attitude to their writing between George MacDonald and many of his contemporaries. While others often wrote what they considered fashionable and acceptable to their readers, George wrote what his heart and soul directed. Consequently his first significant novel *David Elginbrod* was rejected by Smith Elder & Co. and several other publishers, and had it not been for a recommendation from Miss Mulock, the author of *John Halifax, Gentleman* George's career as a novelist might never have got any further. As it was Hurst & Blackett accepted *David Elginbrod* and it was published in 1863. It received immediate recognition and proved one of MacDonald's most popular novels.

The book is most remarkable for its characterisation. David Elginbrod himself, the old Scottish bailiff, is based on George's own father. It is in his extempore prayers that the old crofter is most eloquent. They express an authentic personal relationship with God, so different from the formal stereotyped approach of the average minister. The appropriate setting for the simple cottar and his wife and daughter — the old stone cottage with its welcoming hearth, before which a humble meal of tatties and milk supped from a horn spoon and shared with typical highland hospitality, is convincingly described. By contrast with this scene of natural goodness there is the shallow conventional household of an English Lord at Arnstead Manor, where every kind of dubious practice, including mesmerism and occultism is being clandestinely pursued by Funkelstein and his associates. Then the scene changes once again. In London, the character of Robert Falconer, a physician and social worker who was to appear in several of MacDonald's books is introduced and he in turn discovers a certain vicar of a London Church who is eulogised as representing George's great friend F.D. Maurice. In Harry, the boy whom Hugh Sutherland tutors, the earliest example of George MacDonald's sensitive and delightfully natural child portraits is to be found.

John Ruskin was one of the first to applaud *David Elginbrod*. In a letter dated June 30th, 1863 he wrote that it was full of 'noble things and beautiful little sentences'.

After George's move to London he became acquainted with several men whose strongly held and original ideas were already influencing the contemporary scene. One of those was John Ruskin, five years his senior. George MacDonald met him at a lecture given at his home, Tudor Lodge, Regents Park in 1863. He was introduced to Ruskin by Mrs la Touche, the mother of Rose with whom Ruskin was in love. Ruskin was upset at the time because his articles entitled 'Munera Pulveris' which denigrated the economic policies of the government concerning housing were rejected as impracticable and unacceptable. Three years later we find Ruskin as a frequent visitor at the MacDonalds' house at Hammersmith, 'The Retreat', to which they had moved in 1867. By this time Ruskin had become a great friend of MacDonald even giving him financial help in 1866. George however insisted on repaying the sum, whereupon Ruskin, equally determined, retaliated by giving Louisa a piano. It was at The Retreat that Ruskin used to meet his beloved Rose whom he had known since her childhood. His mother strongly disapproved of the attachment on the grounds of the disparity in their ages – Rose being seventeen to Ruskin's fifty when he first proposed to her. There was also a hint of scandal in the opposition owing to a rumour that Ruskin's first marriage had been a failure on account of his supposed impotence. The affair lasted for ten years ending only with Rose's death in 1872. There had been no impropriety in their relationship. Rose was a sweet girl and Ruskin's an honourable and genuine love. He had confided in his friend about the cause of the breaking up of his marriage and George MacDonald trusted him as he makes clear in a letter. He did all he could therefore to bring them together, but Rose was delicate and could not stand up to the opposition of her parents. She returned his last letter unopened, perhaps because of some slanderous gossip about his marriage, and Ruskin never recovered from the hurt.

Ruskin formed an attachment to MacDonald as a reaction to the rejection of his ideas on industrialism but the friendship was gradually built up on mutual interests. In John Ruskin he found a sympathetic ear for his theories.

Ruskin's great contribution to the life and thought of his time had its origin in his love of beauty. From childhood he had developed an extreme sensitivity to colour, line and form as it was presented to him in nature. His appreciation of it was more than aesthetic; it was an expression of morality also. To him ugliness was an offence against the universe and a symptom of human fallibility. In later life he became active in the cause of stemming the tide of pollution in the countryside and was fully in sympathy with the views of Octavia Hill which led to the formation of the National Trust. In *Sesame and Lilies* he deplores the fact that while daughters are taught to think only of their own beauty 'the pleasant places which God made at once for their school room and their playground lie desolate and defiled'. From beauty in nature Ruskin turned to the question of architecture. He believed that drab, vulgar and inconvenient buildings were caused by an attitude of mind in those who plan and actually build them. In the case of the former the fault lay in a laissez-faire approach and a desire to obtain the greatest profit from the enterprise. With the latter, the trouble stemmed from a total lack of pride in their work and even dislike of it. The remedy he maintained lay in a new approach towards educating the working man, who given a chance, had just as great an intellectual capacity as those from more privileged backgrounds. By the establishment of working Men's Colleges they might be brought actually to enjoy their work instead of regarding it merely as a means of making money. In Ruskin's view such enterprises should be financed by the wealthy who should regard it as their responsibility to provide for the needs of the poor. His theories were expressed in a series of lectures entitled 'To This Last' and based on the biblical parable of the labourers in the Vineyard. Ruskin was looking towards a welfare state, but one financed not by the government but by the wealthy and privileged.

In all this George MacDonald found himself in agreement with his friend. He himself had known poverty at first hand which Ruskin had not and he was as concerned as his friend about the appalling housing conditions in London and elsewhere with whole families crowded into a single room or forced to live like rats in cellars without water or sanitation, the victims of disease and death. In his novel *Weighed and Wanting*, published in 1880, which shows the influence of Ruskin's socialistic ideas and work, he condemns the landlords who exploit their tenants and refuse to maintain their properties. In *Robert Falconer* published in 1868, MacDonald paints a picture of poverty, degradation and squalor in the slums of London equalled only by Dickens in its lurid detail.

> In the gin palaces for example were ragged women who took their half-dead babies from their bare, cold cheerless bosoms and gave them of the poison of which they themselves drank renewed despair in the name of comfort. And the little clay-coloured baby faces made a grimace or two and sank to sleep on the thin tawny breasts of their mothers. Where do they all go when the gin-halls close their yawning jaws? Where do they lie down at night? In the charnel vaults of pestiferously crowded lodging houses, in the prisons of police stations, under dry arches within hoardings.

Like Robert Owen, Ruskin believed that living in sordid conditions prevented human beings from growing to their full moral and intellectual stature, so he bought up slum property and arranged for it to be repaired and made habitable and he influenced other wealthy friends to do the same. In one instance which MacDonald fictionalises in *Robert Falconer* certain friends, Lord and Lady Ducie in particular, forced an undertaker who owing to the nature of his business made capital out of his tenant during their life as well as after their death, to give up the lease of his property which was subsequently handed over to Octavia Hill for her housing project. But George did not agree that environment was the deciding factor in people's moral development. In *Robert Falconer* he queries whether children would be happier if suddenly removed to strange, salubrious surroundings but without an experience of personal love and concern from someone who really cared. MacDonald tended to put the application of Christian love and evangelism before philanthropy and social service.

In his attempts to right social evils and make the world a better place for all levels of society, Ruskin tended to look back, not forward. His ideal for architecture derived from the medieval period and his political economy was based on the 'good old days' of the feudal system. For this reason he was against industrialism and scientific progress. He deplored the spoilation of the countryside by the building of factories, making of canals and construction of railways. In a letter to MacDonald he bemoans the fact that men are 'making hells of their great towns with steam, avarice, cruelty and accursed labour'. In his opinion it was degrading to a man to be subject to the laws of machinery instead of being free to create with his own hands. He did not really believe in progress and utterly rejected Darwin's evolutionary theories. Nature, he felt, should be accepted for what it is in all its beauty, proportion and intricate detail, and above all in its power to enlighten and inspire.

MacDonald on the other hand could not agree with his friend's attitude to industrialism. He believed that progress is inherent in the scheme of things — 'there is no standing still' as Hester observed to Miss Vivasour in *Weighed and Wanting*, 'nothing has ever stopped yet'. For this reason MacDonald was able to accept Darwinism without losing faith in the revelation of truth to be found in the Scriptures.

Ruskin had given up Christianity in 1860. He found much that was distasteful in the doctrines and organization of the Church of England. He disliked the rivalry and back-biting which existed among various denominations and justified his own lack of enthusiasm by blaming Christians for their un-Christian behaviour. In spite of a fundamentally Christian upbringing, as he was nurtured on the bible, Ruskin finalised his abandonment of Christianity by questioning the very existence of God. So accustomed was he by training and inclination to rely on his senses to scrutinize every phenomenon that he could not believe in the necessity of faith. It was his duty, he stated in a letter to George 'to believe nothing but what we know to be fact'. MacDonald's answer on the question of proving God's existence was to deny the possibility of any scientific proof. He declared that he could not believe in a God who could be defined according to the measurements of a man's limited mind and experience but only by the power of faith which transcends mind and fact. The love and truth of God he believed could be conveyed to the human spirit by the power of the imagination through the many varied experiences of life − in the beauty of nature, the love of parent, wife or child, in the joys and sorrows of human life.

Both Ruskin and MacDonald had the capacity for pantheistic experience. MacDonald describes his reaction on confronting the Jungfrau for the first time in *Wilfrid Cumbermede*, (1872). Ruskin, in *Praeterita*, an autobiographical volume published towards the end of his life, records the same experience − an uplifting of the heart and soul, a kind of transfiguration. For Ruskin its snow-clad beauty was 'an instinctive awe mingled with delight... a perception of sanctity in the whole of nature, a pleasure infinitely greater than any which has since been possible....comparable in intensity only to the joy of a lover in being near a noble and kind mistress, but no more explicable or definable than that feeling of love itself '. MacDonald sees it more pictorially

> the clouds broken into a mighty window through which looked in upon him [Wilfrid Cumbermede] a huge mountain peak swathed in snow. One great level band of darker cloud crossed its breast, above which rose the peak triumphant in calmness and stood unutterably solemn and grand in clouds as white as its own whiteness.... with a sudden sweep the clouds curtained the mighty window and the Jungfrau withdrew into its Holy of Holies.... but from the mind it glorified it has never vanished... I had seen something which raised me above my former self and made me long to rise higher yet.

This was George MacDonald's own experience on his first visit to Switzerland in 1865 and he records it through the eyes of Wilfrid Cumbermede seven years later.

The 'Jungfrau' experience shows that although Ruskin set so

much store by facts and the outward and visible image of natural objects, he was avowedly open to spiritual experience and of this MacDonald reminded him when they were discussing the place of proof in human experience. Considering the basic difference in their outlook and the fact that their temperaments were very different — Ruskin fiery and volatile and MacDonald quieter, more serene and patient, it is perhaps surprising that these two men should have had so warm a relationship. Fortunately they had the capacity to discuss and disagree amicably and at the same time to respect the other's point of view. Basically they had the same vision and aspiration to redeem society, but whereas Ruskin was concerned with the welfare of the population as a whole, MacDonald sought the salvation of the individual soul. While Ruskin aimed at inspiring mankind and beautifying and improving his environment, so producing a right attitude to life and work, MacDonald's ideal was that the world should be divinised by knowledge of the presence of God in every creature through the Incarnation.

Ruskin and MacDonald had mutual respect for each other's creative work. George might even have envied the beauty of the language in which *Modern Painters* for example is written. Ruskin's letter to his friend on the publication of *Unspoken Sermons* in 1868 illustrates how admiration survived the important differences in their outlook and belief:

Dear MacDonald,

Thank you exceedingly for the book. They are the best sermons — beyond all compare — I have ever read, and if sermons did good, these will. Pages 23, 24 are very beautiful — unspeakably beautiful. If they were but true... But I feel so strongly that it is only the image of your own mind that you see in the sky! And you will say, "And who made the mind?" Well, the same hand that made the adder's ear — and the tiger's heart — and they shall be satisfied when they awake — with their likeness. It is a precious book though — God give you grace of it.

Above all perhaps, both men had this in common: they were artists actuated by imagination in their perception of the truth, possessing a Wordsworthian power 'to see into the life of things'. Ruskin called it instinct and MacDonald, imaginative vision. It could be given through seeing a lovely flower or hearing the song of birds. To Ruskin this was probably the nearest he could get to an idea of heaven, but to George MacDonald it was a sign of the immanence of God and a promise of immortality, 'bright shoots of everlastingness'.

Another acquaintance of this period was the Rev. C.L. Dodgson better known as Lewis Carroll. George MacDonald had met him first at Hastings. Dodgson was a distinguished mathematician at Christ Church, Oxford. He had been ordained deacon in the Church of England but was never priested, possibly because he had an unfortunate stammer. While the MacDonalds were at Hastings George met Dodgson through a mutual friend, a homeopath, Dr Hale who put Dodgson in touch with a philologist and stammer-curer, James Hunt. They became great friends and Lewis Carroll being a great lover of children, was delighted to make the acquaintance of the little MacDonalds.

Dodgson first encountered Mary MacDonald and her brother Greville aged six at the studio of the sculptor Alexander Munro in 1860 where Greville was posing for the marble statue of Boy with the Dolphin, the fountain in Hyde Park. Dodgson teasingly suggested to Greville that a marble head would be preferable to his own because he would never have to comb his hair! The little boy thought that an excellent idea but when Dodgson pointed out that a marble head couldn't speak, he changed his mind. When the family moved to London, Carroll used to visit them and once took the children to an entertainment at the Haymarket Theatre, and on another occasion to the Coliseum for the great panorama of London. They went with him also to Cremers toy-shop and he fed them on bath-buns and ginger beer. They remembered him with great affection as a kind uncle. Indeed they called him Uncle Dodgson. His stories enchanted them. In his reminiscences of a specialist (1932) Greville recalls

'Uncle Dodgson's method was more potent than he knew, and it made him very dear to us. We would climb about him as with pen and ink, he sketched absurd or romantic or homely incidents, the while telling us their stories with no moral hints to spoil their charm....Then he would take us to that old home of delight the polytechnic to see the 'dissolving views' of Christmas Fairy Tales...

There was a toy-shop in Regent Street where he let us choose gifts
one of which will remain my own as long as memory endures. It was
an unpainted, wooden horse. I loved it as much as any girl her doll...

Carroll was constantly inviting the whole family to spend the day
with him at Oxford, but they do not appear to have done so. Some
of his letters to Louisa and the children are extant. They show his
genuine love of children and ability to identify himself with their
interests. In a letter to Mary MacDonald he expresses a wish to see
them all and also their kitten Snowdrop, whom he immortalises in
the first chapter of *Alice Through the Looking-glass*. In another he
thanks her for sending a sonnet she has written and as a friend of the
family, wrote to congratulate Mary on her engagement to E.R.
Hughes.

Carroll was also a keen and competent photographer. He
photographed George MacDonald with some of his children in their
home in December 1863. Later on he attended the theatrical
performances such as *Pilgrim's Progress, Snow White* and *Blue-
Beard* which Louisa MacDonald used to produce with the whole
family taking part.

On one of his visits to the family Lewis Carroll asked George to
try out the MS of *Alice in Wonderland* on the children. Louisa
therefore read the story to them and according to Greville it was
enthusiastically received.

'When she came to the end, I being aged six exclaimed that there
ought to be sixty thousand volumes of it. Certainly it was our
enthusiasm that persuaded Uncle Dodgson as we called him to
present the English-speaking world, with one of its future classics'.
There was mutual appreciation between the authors, Carroll telling
Mary MacDonald in a letter of January 1866 that he had just read
Alec Forbes and thinks Annie Anderson one of the nicest heroines
'when you get used to the Scots'. He quoted one of George
MacDonald's poems 'Lessons for a Child' in a letter to Ellen Terry
in March 1883 which expresses a romantic pantheism. George on
his side advised Carroll about an illustrator for *Alice Through the
Looking-Glass*, and gave him a letter of introduction to Sir Noel
Paton as a possible artist who unfortunately refused on the grounds

of health.

Carroll appreciated Louisa's sense of humour and she his. On one occasion he went with her and Lily, the eldest MacDonald daughter, to call on Mrs Kate Lewis nee Terry by appointment but found her out, whereupon Carroll wrote an amusing letter to Lilia purporting to be from Mrs Terry inventing preposterous reasons as to why she was not at home.

Moray Lodge
Sunday May 22 1869

My dear Mr Dodgson

I think I had better tell you candidly my reasons for being absent when you called with Miss Lily MacDonald. Before making her acquaintance I felt it right to make a few enquiries, in order to be sure whether or no it would be desirable to meet her. With this object I put the matter into the hands of an experienced detective officer Inspector Pollaky who kindly undertook to make out all about her.... I grieve to tell you that he has discovered her to be mean, vindictive and barbarious to a degree you will hardly credit.

But I will give the painful particulars as Mr Pollaky has just been here: his head and shoulders covered with earth, and he was altogether so shaken and confused that I had some difficulty in making out his story....

It appears that he got into the garden behind the 'Retreat' (your friend's house) disguised as a clothes-horse (I asked him how this was done but could not understand his explanation, beyond the fact that he had a blue apron over his head). He then proceeded to make observations through the dining-room window where Mrs. LMD was superintending the meal of her younger children. He declares that after watching a minute or two, he saw her seize an unoffending chicken, plunge a fork into the poor thing and with a sharp knife cut off its wings and legs. He was so horrified at this barbarity that he fainted and fell headlong into the flower-bed where he was found half buried by Mr MacDonald who however let him go on his explaining that he was trying to find his way to the Underground railway. I asked him if he was sure the chicken was alive to which he replied with tears in his eyes 'If I hadn't been do you think I should have fell that sudden?' which convinced me.

I trust that you will take warning by this and have no more to do with such a wretch.
Believe me
Sincerely yours, Kate Lewis

Mrs Lewis's actual note of apology stated that she was out in her open pony carriage when a sudden shower of rain forced her to take shelter and delayed her return. But the fabricated apology is a good example of the inventive absurdity of Dodgson's humour.

It was not only on a literary plane that those two writers met. They had much more in common than admiration of each other's work. George greatly appreciated Carroll's humour, his ridicule of triteness and hypocrisy in the world of morals, as well as education both through the written word and also in his illustrations, although these were not actually used in the book when published, but those of Tenniel. But at a deeper level they had, more importantly, a similar philosophy of life. Both were intensely sincere in their religious beliefs though not of the same persuasion. Dodgson was a staunchly middle-of-the-road Anglican, whereas MacDonald was equally staunch in not allowing himself to be put into a category although by this time favouring in practice the high Anglican tradition upheld by his friend F.D. Maurice. Both men were blessed with a tremendously fertile imagination which each used to create in his writing a dream world, but they did not do so for the same reason. Initially Carroll's wonderland came into being fortuitously to amuse the Liddell children, but eventually as his writing grew in importance in his life, it became an escape from the dusty academic life of Oxford. MacDonald on the other hand believed his world of faerie to be the real world in which he could help his readers to escape from unreality and find the true meaning of life. But they were alike in believing in the sanctity of childhood and they were able to recreate a world which was credible to children and acceptable to adults too.

In his children's books, MacDonald was writing to make holiness and goodness attractive to children, but also to give them a challenge because only through great and noble adventures do his characters win through to their goal. That message could be appreciated by adults as well. They can learn, for instance, in *The Princess and Curdie* how a false sense of superiority and power in industrial life can tyrannize the population in general and threaten its ultimate prosperity. George wrote to entertain children as well as to instruct, but for him there was no dichotomy between the two. Dodgson on

89

the other hand has a didactic intention, but it was secondary to his desire to amuse his little friends. In an 'Easter Greeting to Every Child Who Loves Alice', in 1876 he wrote 'If I have written anything to add to those stories of innocent and healthy amusement that are laid up in books for the children I love so well, it is surely something I may hope to look back upon without shame or sorrow... when my turn comes to walk through the valley of shadows'.

MacDonald wrote also to dispel the illusion of class distinctions, by showing that it was a person's character which determined whether he were a gentleman or no. As far as his own family was concerned George MacDonald seemed devoid of social ambition. As Greville recalls, his father once said, 'he would make me a watchmaker, as my hands were better than my head; and he would have been quite as proud of a son if he proved a first-rate craftsman, I think, as a luminary in any profession'. Carroll on the other hand, whose background was Harrow and Oxford tended to perpetuate such hierarchies.

Fundamentally Lewis Carroll was as serious-minded as George MacDonald in directing the course of his life. When he resigned his mathematical lectureship he wrote in his diary, 'I shall now have my whole time at my disposal, and if God give life and continued health and strength may hope...to do some worthy work in writing, partly in the cause of innocent recreation for children and partly I hope in the cause of religious thought. May God bless the new form of life that lies before me that I may use it according to His holy will' and to that prayer his friend George would surely have said 'Amen'.

New Scenes
New Faces

In July 1862 a third son Robert Falconer was born, bringing the total number of MacDonald children up to eight. The family had by this time moved from Tudor Lodge in Regents Park to Earles Terrace near Kensington High Road. It was thought it would prove a more healthy locality for MacDonald who was still suffering intermittently from bronchitis and asthma. He continued his lecures in the new house which was more conveniently situated for those who attended.

In 1865 George went for a holiday in Switzerland with William Matheson. He was tremendously impressed en route with the scenery and architecture, especially with Antwerp Cathedral with its magnificent spire, and in spite of his asthma insisted on climbing every one of the six hundred and sixteen steps. At Basle he repeated the experiment and climbed the spire. Here he was greatly taken with a clock which re-enacted the church's festivals and myths of various kinds with goddesses and performing horses and chariots. At Thun he saw dancing in the streets which were decorated with green boughs like the English traditional Maytime ritual of Jack in the Green. The highlight of the tour was the sight of the Jungfrau wrapped in clouds, so vividly described in *Wilfrid Cumbermede*. In a letter to his wife from Murren he describes his feeling of exaltation on viewing the Jungfrau: 'I am much better dear, (He had been suffering from Lumbago) I have been out a good part of the afternoon. And if I had seen nothing else, I could now go home content. Yet I am not sure whether amidst the lovely chaos of shifting clouds I have seen the highest peak of the Jungfrau. It is utterly useless to describe it... I hate the photographs, they convey no idea. The tints and the lines and the mass and the streams and vapours and the mingling and the infinitude and the loftiness, the glaciers and the slow crawling avalanches — they cannot be described.

Once today, looking through the mist I said with just a slight reservation of doubt in my heart, there that is as high as I want it to be, and straight way I saw a higher point grow out of the mist beyond. So I have found it with all the ways of God. And so will you too, dear love.... He felt the stirring of pantheistic belief and was 'filled with the vague recognition of a present soul in nature with the sense of the humanity everywhere diffused through her and operating upon ours'. Its varied loveliness Wilfrid declares 'would take the soul of a Wordsworth or a Ruskin to comprehend or express'.

MacDonald wrote *Wilfrid Cumbermede* about seven years after his visit to Switzerland as a tribute to his friend John Ruskin who by that time had been rejected by Rose la Touche, and through whom he had been introduced to the experience of the Alps.

The year after his return from Switzerland George's fourth son Maurice, called after his friend and mentor was born, and the year after Bernard Powell. The MacDonalds were devoted to their children, and like typical Victorian parents seem to have had no idea of limiting the size of their family. George in fact regretted that he had failed as a parent in stopping short of a dozen. The eleventh child, a boy, was born in 1867. George and Louisa regarded each of their children as a miraculous gift from God and saw in their individuality some aspect of the character of their maker. Although they were brought up quite strictly and had little formal education, the MacDonald children throve in the atmosphere of love and devotion to God and absorbed the culture which was so liberally provided by their father through his lectures and the many thoughtful and original people who came to the house. Through his own writing, George taught them to be receptive to the truth. *Magic and Mystery* Greville MacDonald declares 'nonsense and fun did more for us than moral precept or standardized education'.

The next ten years, 1865 to 1875, were to see a tremendous

increase in George MacDonald's literary output. No less than nine novels were published as well as three books for children. Several of them appeared in serial form in periodicals such as the *Argosy*, *Good Words* and the *Sunday Magazine*. Among the novels were *Alec Forbes* and *Malcolm*, two Scottish stories which are by many considered amongst his best.

But at the same time he was developing his academic work. He applied in 1865 for the Chair of English Literature at Edinburgh University. Among those who supported his application was John Ruskin whose testimonial was as follows: 'I am always glad to hear you lecture myself and if I had a son I would rather he took lessons in literary taste under you than under any person I know, for you would make him more than a scholar – a living and thoughtful reader'. But George did not get the post in spite of his reputation as a lecturer, probably because he was known to have, from a Presbyterian standpoint, heretical views.

In 1867 the MacDonald family spent the summer at Bude in Cornwall. The party included Octavia Hill, the founder of the National Trust, who had been working hard in London trying to put into practice Ruskin's idealistic ideas about housing the poor and restoring Paradise Row, Marylebone, which he had bought for the project. Octavia was badly in need of a rest and holiday. She earned her keep by coaching Greville daily in Latin, weather permitting, on the top of Chapel Rock.

In *The Sea Board Parish* George MacDonald describes their arrival at Bude, thinly disguised as Kilkhaven. They went part of the way by train as far as the borders of Devonshire, and then on by post-chaise, a five hour journey in an open carriage which gave them the maximum opportunity of enjoying the scenery. It was a hilly journey and hard work for the horses. The winding road provided the joy of the unexpected, the scene constantly changing and the scents which wafted towards them drowning even the pungent smell of the horses; the flower-scented breath of summer in cottage gardens as they passed, the smell of burning wood, of peat smoke from the chimneys fragrance of new-mown hay and the acrid aroma of pines. As they passed over Dartmoor, golden here and there with gorse and patches of purple heather not yet in flower, George would have been reminded of his beloved Huntly. As they came near the sea a fresh west wind was blowing, laden with salt spray from the crested waves. The landscape was barer now with only an occasional tree bending landwards flattened by the wind. Then the road began to lead down in gradual decline to sea level, and they came in sight of the village of Kilkhaven. In *The Seaboard Parish* the house where the Waltons were staying was The Old Rectory. It was approached over a bridge spanning the river, the road then followed the stream and over another wooden drawbridge by the side of a canal where sloops and schooners were riding at anchor. The Rectory was perched on rocks above the breakwater and to the landward side of the house were the downs, the soft springy turf with a scattering of wild flowers, yellow ragwort, toadflax, clover and knapweed yielding a delicate fragrance beneath the pressure of footsteps.

Although the Walton family's abode in *The Seaboard Parish* is called The Old Rectory, the MacDonalds actually stayed at the last two cottages on the Quay almost at the water's edge, corresponding exactly to the description in that book. They were built into the rocky wall and when the tide was high and the sea stormy the cottages were covered in spray. They had originally been converted from fish cellars which accounted for the semi-underground character of some of the rooms. The MacDonald's cottages adjoined the residence of Sir Thomas Acland and were owned by him. All three are now incorporated in what is called to-day Efford Cottage. The Aclands owned much of the property in Bude and were liberal landlords. Sir Thomas, the tenth Baronet, who was in his eightieth year in 1867 when the MacDonalds were staying there, was the first to conceive the idea that Bude might become a sea-side resort. He had the first bathing pool constructed. It was called Sir Thomas Pit and is still in use to-day at the end of the breakwater. He was a strong supporter of the Canal project opened in 1823, to transport goods inland before the coming of the railway and to export goods from the port of Bude. He gave some of the material for the canal, built the Falcon Hotel as a Coaching Inn, and a row of cottages facing the canal for the canal workers. He also gave some land for the building of a lifeboat house opposite the Falcon. The canal flourished for thirty to forty years, heavy goods being brought by sailing ships to the Harbour and then distributed by barges inland on the waterway. With the coming of the railway, trade gradually declined.

The other principal landlord in Bude was the Thynne family who owned much of the land on the east side of the canal. They provided a site for the building of the Bewd Inn or Bude Hotel on the spot where Barclays Bank now is. The living of Kilkhampton a few miles away was in the family's gift and when George MacDonald visited the Church he made the acquaintance of the Revd the Honourable Christopher Thynne. Although the incumbent, he lived at his family seat Penstowe, instead of at the Rectory. The two became friends and George seemed greatly impressed with Kilkhampton Church and in *The Seaboard Parish* he identifies it with Kilkhaven Church of which Mr Walton is locum tenens.

The tremendous power of the sea made a deep impression on George MacDonald and his whole family, for the Atlantic waters rise higher at Bude than at any place along the Cornish coast and their roar can be heard many miles away.

During their stay they had plenty of opportunity of realising the sea's cruelty. They saw a drowned man being dragged from the water and may also have witnessed a shipwreck. Such were all too common along that rocky jagged coast. The wreck of the *Uncle John* carrying coal from Newport, took place on the rocks outside Bude breakwater in June of that year and MacDonald has given a graphic description of a wreck in *The Seaboard Parish*. Another incident in that book as related by Mr Walton, which may have been MacDonald's own experience, describes how he and two other people narrowly escaped drowning when they were stranded on the far side of the breakwater near Chapel Rock. They managed to survive by throwing themselves on the stones of the breakwater so that the huge waves did not dash them to pieces but burst over them floating them up from the stones where they lay. When they finally got across and saw an enormous wave sweep the breakwater from end to end, they realised how near to death they had been.

95

But when the sea was in a quieter, kindlier mood, and the waves were gentle, George delighted in dashing across the breakwater carrying his two youngest boys, one under each arm, in order to beat the tide.

While they were at Bude, the MacDonalds visited the majestic, remotely situated church of Morwenna at Morwenstowe, set near towering cliffs four hundred feet above the sea on a wild and rugged part of the coast. They met its eccentric poet-Vicar Robert Stephen Hawker, and received a great welcome from the old priest and his wife Pauline, forty years younger than himself. His first wife Charlotte had died four years previously. They had a baby of a few months called Morwenna. After a sumptuous Cornish tea with thick cream and strawberry jam, taken in the beautiful rectory which Hawker had designed himself, MacDonald and Hawker had a good talk and found they had much in common. Both were poets and they were not unlike in character: each fearlessly holding his own views regardless of the criticism of others. They were both flamboyant in their dress, exhibiting perhaps, some of the vanity of other mortals. Hawker, as did MacDonald with his kilt of bright tartan and Scotch bonnet, made a striking and somewhat outlandish figure. Instead of the conventional clerical black or grey, Hawker favoured a magenta cassock, yellow poncho and fisherman's boots and jersey. On his head he wore a pink, felt, brimless hat, the normal headgear so he maintained of an Armenian Archimandrite. His whole appearance must have astounded the MacDonald children. But George would have perceived the kind and compassionate nature of the man and his deep love for his parishioners even when they professed Methodism which he, being High Church, abominated. But Hawker was almost a legend by this time in his work of seeking to rescue, at great personal risk, the bodies of sailors wrecked on the cruel jagged rocks at Morwenstowe and giving them a Christian burial in his churchyard. Then there was a love of animals which they had in common. Hawker was devoted to his pony, Carrow, which he harnessed to a trap and drove over hill and dale to the remotest corners of his parish. He had a pet pig, Gyp, who was house-trained and groomed regularly and 'lived as family'. Dogs and cats were welcome to attend church servcies. Like George MacDonald, Hawker hoped for and believed in their immortality.

The MacDonalds had made the journey in a wagonette drawn by two horses. On the way home the horses jibbed at mounting Coombe Hill till re-assured by George who had a gift for managing and understanding animals.

Another time they went to Tintagel and made the perilous climb to the Castle which in 1867 must have been even more hazardous than to-day. But there was no need for them to go far afield for entertainment. The port of Bude was busy with plenty of shipping. During the summer of 1867 over one hundred vessls docked in the harbour bringing a variety of merchandise. The chief commodities imported were coal and manure. Then there were the barges which distributed the in-coming cargoes throughout Cornwall by way of the Canal – north to Tavistock, east to Blagdon Moor and south to Droxton near Launceston. The Bude Harbour and Canal Company traded its own cargo of sea-sand which was much in demand as a fertiliser for acid soil. It was collected from the beach in tub-boats which ran along rails between the shore and the canal lock and were drawn by cart horses, but the development of chemical fertilisers gradually diminished the trade.

Then there was the excitement of the launching of the lifeboat, a very laborious task – and an all too frequent event – even allowing for practices. A new lifeboat house on the canal opposite the Falcon Hotel was most picturesque, but the launching of the boat was a hazardous affair. Weather permitting, it was floated down through the lock gates and placed on launching carriages drawn by ten cart horses which dragged it into the sea. The crew looked very smart in their red caps and blue and white tunics, but many of them were destined to lose their lives. The fictitious Mr Walton tries to alert the crew when a severe storm blows up and a ship is foundering at the entrance to the harbour, by ringing the church bell, but it is too late to save the thirteen people on board for whom he has the sad task of arranging the burial.

Other diversions were of a more cheerful nature – picnics and bathing on the beach and peaceful walks on Summerleaze Down. In all these MacDonald joined in light-heartedly with his family and friends and no doubt played a leading role in making the holiday for all concerned a happy time to remember. Greville testified to this in his autobiography of his parents: 'Those days in Bude remain in my mind as the happiest of all my childhood holidays; and chiefly because our father inspite of his indefatigable writing took more share in our romps and pleasures than I ever remember. Then closer because more light-hearted, friendship with some of our parents, friends was possible and certainly made our happiness'.

On their return from Cornwall the MacDonalds moved from Earles Terrace to a Georgian house fronting the river at Hammersmith. It was at that time called The Retreat, but after William Morris had lived there it was re-named Kelmscott House as it is still known to-day.

The Retreat had a large garden of nearly an acre, stabling, a lawn and a shrubbery. It soon became a centre for literary gatherings. Many friends and visitors found their way to The Retreat especially on the day of the boat race. There was room here for entertaining on a larger scale. They had a stage erected on the lawn hung with curtains where Louisa produced little plays mostly of a fairy nature in which her children could take part. Performances were given annually to poor tenants from Octavia Hill's housing estate. Distinguished guests would also patronize them, such as Tennyson, Ruskin, the Burne-Joneses, Lewis Carroll and the Revd Samuel Barrett, founder of Toynbee Hall. The MacDonald children thoroughly enjoyed these occasions. Sometimes they played the piano or violin to amuse the guests, or would unobtrusively mingle with the crowd and drink in snatches of conversation. They learned a lot from observing their elders and did not expect special attention from their parents. After the play refreshments would be served and dancing followed. Ruskin and Octavia Hill on one occasion partnered each other for Sir Roger de Coverley. Sometimes Octavia's 'poor' got more to eat than the distinguished guests.

It was not only for entertainment that Octavia's tenants were invited to meet George MacDonald. He used to preach on Sundays at Octavia's refuge for them at Barrett's Court near to Wigmore Street, and aroused their interest and gained their confidence. Where possible the MacDonalds would employ them about the house and grounds. George was happy in this little community of Christian Socialism. He kept open house for tea and supper on Sunday and everyone joined in the washing-up.

Outside all was beauty as MacDonald describes in a letter: 'the shining river and the white-sailed boats with the wind tossing the rosy hawthorn before my windows and the magnolia trained up the wall looking in at one of them'. Inside his study the walls were lined with books and at one end, taking up about one third of the room, was a stage with curtains. An artist friend had decorated the room with crimson wall paper, stencilled with black fleur de lis and the ceiling was a dark blue studded with silver stars and a crescent moon. George loved bright colours. Their first performance of *The Pilgrims Progress* took place here in 1877.

In 1875 the house next door, River Villa, was added to the establishment and two young girls, daughters of Richard Cobden, joined the household. It was a happy-go-lucky atmosphere with everyone having a part to play and an unselfish one at that. George's great friend, William Carey-Davies, a former student at Kings College whose faith he had helped to restore, acted as his secretary. During the years 1868 to 1875 his writing was going on apace and Davies was a great help in reading the proofs.

Another original thinker of whom George MacDonald made a great friend during this London period was the Christian Socialist Frederick Dennison Maurice. Maurice was an Anglican theologian whom MacDonald first met in 1854 at the opening of a Working Men's College when Maurice gave the inaugural address. Maurice had become involved in an experiment to establish such a college in a house in Red Lion Square. As its first Principal he was responsible for drawing up a scheme of organization and the project had attracted some men of outstanding talent such as John Ruskin who taught drawing there, and Dante Gabriel Rosetti painting.

George was impressed with Maurice's address and the conviction which it expressed that God is to be sought in every pursuit, not

merely in something technically called religion. Although he had not
previously met Maurice his name was well known to all who took
theological matters seriously, for the previous year 1853, Maurice
had been dismissed from the post of Professor of Theology at the
newly established King's College in London after he had refused to
resign for teaching what the Council called 'dangerous doctrines
contrary to those of the Church of England' and 'calculated to upset
the minds of theological students'. Maurice had published a series of
Theological Essays, one of which, on Eternal Life, repudiates the
orthodox belief that God has ordained multitudes of people to eternal
punishment. He maintained that 'eternal life' in St John's Gospel
refers not to its duration but to its quality. Fellowship with God
through knowledge of Him and the word must therefore have the
same meaning when applied to punishment. No-one need be
eternally lost for no-one is outside the love of God, and love is
stronger than death and embraces the whole universe. To the
authorities at King's College and many religious leaders of the
Church who subscribed to the Thirty-Nine Articles, such teaching
was dangerous in suggesting to the ignorant and careless a licence
to sin with impunity.

Not only did MacDonald admire the courage of the man in boldly
declaring the truth as he saw it and standing firm when discredited
in the eyes of his colleagues and students and threatened with the
loss of his job, but he found himself also in great sympathy with
Maurice's views. As a result of that first meeting a deep and lasting
friendship was to develop. By 1863 MacDonald was so well
acquainted with Maurice and so far advanced in the understanding of
his mind and character that he portrayed him in his novel *David
Elginbrod* as a certain enlightened preacher, and the following year
George's fourth son was given the name Maurice as a token of
affection for his friend, and, as a mark of respect for his teaching,
Maurice was asked to be godfather to the child.

In spite of nineteen years difference in their ages, the two had
much in common. Both had had a non-conformist upbringing and had
renounced their cradle beliefs in the cause of sincerity and honesty
and had had the courage to change course in their youth. George had

abandoned the congregational ministry rather than be forced to preach a negative faith which he could not accept and which he believed obscured rather than clarified the gospel message. Later, however, he joined the Church of England on the testimony of his friend, though he would not accept ordination which required subscribing to the Thirty Nine Articles though he did not criticize Maurice for so doing, having perfect confidence in his friend's sincerity.

Maurice on the other hand had started life as a Unitarian. His father was a fanatical Unitarian minister who strove to bring up his children in this narrow creed, but one by one they rejected it, inevitably causing dissension and unhappiness in the family. Maurice was serious-minded even as a boy and longed for the peace and unity denied him in his home life. He vowed at the age of fifteen to lead a good life and benefit mankind. He had leanings towards the Ministry, but the Unitarian belief that he was already destined to eternal damnation held him back. Fortunately at Cambridge he was able to shake off these gloomy thoughts and in the doctrine of the Trinity eventually found the unity and harmony which Unitarianism had denied him, and in the doctrine of the Incarnation which a study of the Johannine Epistles had revealed to him, he found the answer to his search for holiness and knowledge of God. The Church of England with its two Sacraments of life was from then on to him the vehicle by which the Incarnation was made a reality to men, and through which they might share in the very life of God. But Maurice did not immediately become an Anglican. He left Cambridge without taking a degree because to a man of his integrity and independence of thought it seemed unacceptable that he should be forced by the Establishment to be a member of the Church of England before he could be eligible to graduate. But still feeling drawn to the Ministry he finally began his academic life all over again at Oxford and was ordained Deacon in 1834. While accepting the Thirty Nine Articles himself he did not think undergraduates should be forced to pay lip-service to them, but once he had accepted the authority of the church he defended them as providing a guarantee, a standard of beliefs, at a time when liberalism was tending to erode basic teaching. Realising how at what a high price a genuine personal faith may be won, Maurice always respected an individual's creed, but he would not tolerate a watering down or amalgam of the church's teaching which had its origin in expediency or the desire for the sake of peace to accommodate other parties in the church; although he did put his own interpretation on the clause referring to everlasting damnation in the Athanasian Creed.

George MacDonald appreciated Maurice's dilemma in being forced to choose between intellectual honesty and loyalty to the doctrines of the Church based on the revelation of the mind of God in the Incarnation. In a poetical tribute to his friend 'Thanksgiving for F.D. Maurice' he interprets and summarises the essence of his teaching in a verse which was omitted from the published version.

> He taught that hell herself is yet within
> The confines of Thy Kingdom, and its fires
> The endless conflict of Thy love with sin
> That even by horror, works its pure desires.

In *David Elginbrod* MacDonald refers to Maurice's preaching through the testimony of Robert Falconer who attends a Church (St Peter's Vere Street of which Maurice was the incumbent) where the preacher 'looks upon the formularies of the Church of England as utterances of living truth.... He believes entirely that God loves, yea is love and therefore that hell itself is subservient to that love and but an embodiment of it'.

MacDonald's attitude to the Church of England differed from that of his friend. He appreciated it as providing the milieu in which the individual could experience fellowship with God without being subjected to the tyranny of ecclesiasticism as he had experienced in Calvinism, but the church for him was not the only source of revelation. God showed himself to the individual in so far as he was true to his own conscience and open to the vision vouchsafed to him of God 'in primrose, lark and child' for in children, like Diamond in *The Back of the North Wind* and *Sir Gibbie*, is the Kingdom of Heaven to be found.

Both Maurice and MacDonald had philanthropic views of the church. Maurice deplored profiteering and capitalising among its members, yet was aware of the danger of humanitarianism vitiating the teaching of the Creed and watering down the Faith. He wanted the State to work side by side with the Church in applying Christian principles of equality and social justice in legislation with one law for both rich and poor. He believed that philanthropy was not enough and that the Industrial system must be changed. With this in mind Maurice joined with other socially minded Christians such as Carlyle, Ludlow and Vansittart in forming a Christian Socialist Group. One of their first ventures was to start a Co-operative where men were to work without the incentive of personal competitive gain.

While agreeing with the principle of the worth of the individual as a recipient of God's love and concern and the unity of all men as brothers in Christ, George MacDonald could not entirely agree with his friend's socialist aims. To him the responsibility of caring for the individual should be the personal concern of every Christian. He did not care so much about legislation to promote social justice but believed in the obligation of individual Christians to prove the reality of their faith by doing all they could to alleviate social conditions as Hester did in *Weighed and Wanting*. Christopher expresses MacDonald's views on the matter in the same novel. 'I believe in no good done save in person by personal operative presence of soul, body and spirit.... God can use us as tools. How the devil would have laughed at a society for saving the world. But when he saw *one* take it in hand with all his heart and soul who cared for nothing else, then indeed he might tremble for his Kingdom'. The MacDonalds themselves did all they could to help those in need, providing entertainment for them and helping in their education. George MacDonald shared Maurice's spiritual aspirations after social justice but could not follow his practice of it.

But in the final analysis it was the man himself whom MacDonald loved apart from his public or ecclesiastical image, a man of courage who was not afraid to face the truth and act upon it, a humble, sincere and lovable man with a great sense of humour with whom he could share his doubts and hopes and dreams – a friend indeed.

A Decade of Fancy and Imagination

The publication of the fantasy works of George MacDonald which form an important part of his unique contribution to British literature, coincides with a period when his children were reaching an age at which their education had to be taken seriously. At the time of the publication of *At the Back of the North Wind* (1871) and *The Princess and the Goblin* (1872) their ages ranged between five and thirteen years. George was teaching them at home and as he considered the development of imagination to be the most important element in education, it is likely that he tried out these stories first on his own children. The fact that during the years 1869 – 1872 he was editor of *Good Words for The Young* would have facilitated publication. While written for the edification and enjoyment of his own family these stories have continued to be 'best sellers' for adults as well as children ever since.

Juvenile literature in Victorian times had an unashamedly didactic content accepted no doubt by child-readers in the absence of anything more stimulating but MacDonald achieved the same result by an imaginative rather than an authoritarian approach. The child sees the truth by the exercise of his imagination rather than by automatic acceptance of a precept. George MacDonald made goodness attractive because the characters he describes are not goody-goodies or prigs but are rather in the process of becoming good in the seeking of a goal which when it is achieved will make them happy. Their adventures lead them to that goal. For Curdie in *The Princess and Curdie* it was the satisfaction of serving his king at the cost of great danger to himself by rescuing him from evil courtiers who were slowly poisoning him. The little Princess Irene was able to save the life of Curdie, the boy miner, when he was imprisoned by the goblins deep down in the mine, by obediently following the magic thread bestowed upon her by her mysterious great-grandmother; while little Diamond after many adventures with North Wind which tested his courage to the uttermost, found his fulfilment in a happy death at the back of the North Wind.

In *The Princess and the Goblin* the forces of evil are represented by the goblins or cobs who with the aid of their creatures, hideously grotesque caricatures of animals of the natural world, are plotting to undermine the foundations of the castle and capture the Princess Irene. In *The Princess and Curdie*, however, other fabulous creatures of no less horrific appearance under the leadership of Lina, a dog-like beast given to Curdie by great-grandmother as a companion on his dangerous mission, are harnessed by him to overthrow the evil designs of the courtiers of the palace in the decadent city of Gwyntystorm. The resulting narratives are in the tradition of the myths of ancient Greece and fairy stories through the ages. They make thoroughly exciting reading and as such can be enjoyed by children for whom they were originally written.

But they have another dimension which is unique. A purifying wind blows through the pages and with its bracing power shocks the reader and awakens him to reality. The impact is made by the story as a whole or as C.S. Lewis puts it 'the radiance is incarnate in it'; but as George MacDonald himself says, 'every reader will be affected in his own way according to his own nature and development. Your meaning may be superior to mine'. Even children can derive inspiration from being confronted with the attractiveness and power of holiness though they may not understand the symbolism. Yet it is primarily through symbols empowered by his creative imagination that MacDonald expresses his deep Christian convictions regarding the meaning and purpose of life. The fire of roses is perhaps a most striking example. Curdie is directed to thrust his hands into the fire at the cost of almost unbearable pain. The action represented the cleansing which he needed to expiate his wanton shooting of the Princess's pigeon before he set out on his great adventure. This ordeal by fire bestows upon him the ability to know by a hand-shake the true nature of the person he meets. The fire so far from searing his flesh left his hand smooth and white. Curdie's interview with the Princess taught him the truth that it is not good enough to mean no harm as he had pleaded as an excuse for shooting the bird, for 'whoever does not mean good is always in danger'.

MacDonald uses his awareness of the natural world to reveal spiritual truths. To him as to Gerard Manley Hopkins the whole world 'is charged with the grandeur of God' whether it is the vast mountains, 'beautiful terrors', thrown up from the earth by 'a huge power of buried sunlight' or 'the dry withered seed which dibbed in the ground becomes a sweet pea to gladden the heart of the gardener with its delicate colour and exquisite scent, and assure him of resurrection to eternal life'.

MacDonald shows that the natural world must be treated with reverence. The little Princess greeted each flower as it opened. Instead of pulling it she touched it tenderly 'as if it were a new-born baby and having made its acquaintance would leave it as happy as she found it'. He uses the real world as a bridge between earth and heaven — an ordinary staircase led Irene to a meeting with her mysterious great-grandmother.

In his fantasies MacDonald is concerned to show people how to discover the truth which is so often concealed in the outward appearance. He achieves this by presenting to his readers, in the course of the story, a set of values completely opposed to worldly assumptions and conventional ideas. For example great-grandmother does not mind calling herself old. 'It is so silly of people', she tells Irene, 'to fancy that old age means crookedness; feebleness, rheumatism, sticks and forgetfulness. ... the right old age means strength and beauty, mirth and courage, clear eyes and strong painless limbs'. So with poverty: it is a privilege to be poor the old Princess tells Curdie's father, for 'riches are dangerous ... Things come to the poor that can't get in at the door of the rich; their money somehow blocks it up'. On the contrary a man can achieve dignity even though he is hungry and cold, as Peter, Curdie's father was, for it is not these things that degrade a man but 'greed, laziness and selfishness'. Perhaps George was thinking of some of the rich industrialists and capitalists he had known in Manchester and in London who exploited the poor.

It is not easy for adults 'to look to the heart of the matter' for they with their experience and superior knowledge confuse seeing with understanding and are not willing to use their imagination to see the other person's point of view, and perceive the truth. Some people indeed, as Curdie was in danger of doing before his conversion, live their lives on a purely material level and judge by appearances. 'They believe in nothing but their dinner; to be sure of a thing with them is to have it between their teeth'. They are sceptical and cannot see further than their noses like Lootie, the nurse of the little Princess, who scoffed at the child's account of her meeting with her great-grandmother. But George MacDonald is writing for children whose perception is not clouded by wordly wisdom. Their imaginations, still unsullied from birth, are ready to accept with joyful wonder truths which are not obvious except to the pure in heart.

This does not mean that MacDonald believed children to be angels. He had eleven of his own and must have been aware of their less attractive traits. The children to whom he chooses to reveal the way of salvation in his fantasies, Diamond, Curdie and Irene, had their weaknesses — Diamond insists on leaving North Wind to follow the little road-sweeper, Curdie wantonly kills a pigeon and the little Princess is rude to her nurse — but he showed them to be teachable, unprejudiced, uncomplicated and capable of accepting the truth.

George MacDonald's life spanned the greater part of the industrial revolution, at least where its effect on rural existence was concerned. His writing is shot through with reminders of a time when crofting, the market-place, homecraft — above all spinning made up a simple way of life as yet only moderately influenced by industry though there were several looms in Huntly. It is perhaps the happy simplicity of his childhood existence followed by the better experience of urban life for example in industrial Manchester, that provides one of the keys to MacDonald's extraordinary ability to empathise with children.

Although MacDonald's fantasies have the nature and format of fairy stories and as such are still enjoyable to children, their magic arises out of situations which take place in the world of flesh and blood where the characters are human and life-like and their experiences credible. There is no suggestion that the story is merely a dream. The adventures of the little Princess begin when she climbs an ordinary stair in the palace where she lives. In a similar manner C.S. Lewis introduces us to the adventures of the Pevensie children in Narnia by sending them through the back of a very ordinary wardrobe and leaving it to his reader's imagination to follow them through to a magical world. So realistic did the whole adventure seem to one boy who had read *The Lion, The Witch and The Wardrobe* that he was discovered by his parents chopping his way into the back of their wardrobe in an attempt to find the entrance to the Kingdom of Narnia! C.S. Lewis's world which is inhabited by various fabulous beasts including Aslan, the majestic lion, owes much by his own admission, to the faerie romances of George MacDonald, as does J.R.R. Tolkein's early work *The Hobbit* and later saga and sequel *The Lord of the Rings* also to a certain extent show the influence of Lewis's master, though the Professor was loath to admit his indebtedness to MacDonald's writing on account of what he saw to be its didactic content. Yet in spite of his disenchantment with the moral overtones of the MacDonald fantasies, Tolkein shows his affinity to him by admitting that a good fantasy always transmits an experience of joy by presenting the reader with a sudden glimpse of reality or truth whether it is overtly expressed or not. For this reason the 'Fairy Story' found in the gospel he believes to be 'the greatest myth of all for there is no tale ever told that men would rather find was true. It begins and ends with joy'.

As a corollary to this idea it is tempting to speculate whether Professor Tolkein and George MacDonald himself together with his disciple C.S. Lewis would have been unduly disturbed by recent demythologising of gospel traditions and the dismissal by such modern theologians as Bultmann of the miraculous content of the Bible as mere symbolism. For all three are agreed that symbols can be the most powerful medium for conveying truth. The Hobbit's

Bilbo Baggins, the home-loving reluctant dragon hunter and Frodo his nephew, the intrepid guardian of the Ring, are just as much symbols of the highest aspirations of the human spirit as was the initially sceptical Curdie. Bilbo and Frodo are in fact twentieth century knights-errant. 'Hobbits' by definition 'represent people of small imagination but great courage which often leads to survival against all odds'.

But in spite of this common denominator, there is a fundamental difference between Tolkein's purpose in writing and that of his predecessor George MacDonald. Tolkein rejects what he calls MacDonald's 'purposed denomination of his readers' in presenting to them a philosophy of life, a vision of the truth as he, the author, sees it. He prefers an historic basis as preserving the freedom of the reader to interpret the subject according to his own thought and experience.

It is possible to find many casual similarities in the narratives of the two writers: echoes of *Phantastes*, for example, in the personification of trees as exercising an influence, baleful or benign, on those who rest beneath their branches. For MacDonald's Anodos, the Ash was an ogre — 'you will know him by his thick fingers — and the Alder will smother you with her web of hair'. For Tolkein's Pippin, Frodo's companion, the Great Willow turned out to be extremely dangerous — 'his heart was rotten but his strength was green'. In the ghostly 'barrow-wights' which enthralled and terrified Frodo there are links with *Lilith* in the Sleeping Dead shown to Vane by another character, the Raven in the ice-cold mortuary in the house of Adam and Eve.

But these parallels are of minor significance, mere components in the leaf-mould of Tolkein's mind, derived from many sources: *Beowulf* for example, *Gawain and the Green Knight* as well as the Curdie books of George MacDonald. From the rich compost of his reading and worked upon by his imagination, a new Mythology was created, the New World of Middle-earth was born — an imaginary world but utterly convincing and enthralling in a unique way.

In making what he called a 'Secondary' World Professor Tolkein saw himself as a 'sub-creator' deploying his faculties in a Christian manner and 'assisting in the effoliation and multiple enrichment of creation'.

MacDonald's intention though equally Christian was less ambitious. It was simply this: to reveal to his readers the existence of the spiritual world with which he believed the physical universe to be already suffused.

The genius of George MacDonald's fantasy writing does not lie in the inclusion of fantastic creatures and heroes of epic stature who strive with them; for these after all have been an integral feature of mythology from the Minataur of ancient Crete right through to the Tripods and other extra-terrestrial creatures presented on our television screens today. It is rather the breath of other-worldliness pervading every page of his writing, bringing to life the latent desire of his readers to face up to reality, and assuring them of the ultimate triumph of good over evil, which explains the continuing popularity of his fantasies and makes George MacDonald a supreme master of mythopaeic art.

From America to Italy

George MacDonald's reputation as a lecturer and man of letters had by now extended beyond the boundaries of his own country to America. A certain American poet Richard Watson Gilder had become acquainted with George's verse and was greatly attracted to the personality which it suggested. He wrote to MacDonald proposing that he should undertake a lecture tour. Lectures appear to have been even more popular in America at that time than in this country. Dickens and Thackeray had recently returned from such a tour. A lecture bureau in the States was responsible for the arrangements and as the fees were more than favourable, £30 a lecture, a goodly sum in those days, George felt bound to accept for he was still finding it hard to support a growing family on the proceeds of his writing. He was also possibly glad of a change of thought and scene. He had recently suffered the loss of two of his greatest friends: F.D. Maurice and Greville Matheson.

So in September 1872 George and Louisa and their eldest son Greville set sail in the *S.S. Malta* for Boston. The tour was to last six to eight months. They arrived in Boston on September 30th after a smooth passage lasting twelve days, but not smooth enough for poor Louisa. At Boston they stayed with the publisher and writer, James T. Fields and his wife in Charles Street. They were most hospitably entertained. Louisa wrote detailed letters to her children describing the Fields' way of life. The day began with a colossal breakfast consisting of fish, game, omelettes and vegetables, tea, coffee, wine and dessert. Through Fields the MacDonalds were introduced to various writers such as Emerson, Longfellow and Harriet Beecher Stowe. George welcomed the opportunity of meeting people and visiting another country, but found the 'lion-hunters' whom Louisa tried to keep at bay, rather trying.

MacDonald gave his first lecture at Cambridge Port. It was on Burns and lasted one hundred minutes. His eloquent enthusiasm completely captivated his audience, for he spoke without notes and was able to evoke the charm of the ploughman-poet without minimising his faults. Other subjects in his repertoire of lectures included *Hamlet*, Tennyson, *King Lear*, *Macbeth* and Milton, but Burns was generally the most popular.

At Amesbury they visited the Quaker poet Whittier in his simple country cottage. He greatly admired George MacDonald's poetry and revered his spirituality. In fact he wrote a letter to the local press recommending everyone to attend his lectures.

Contemporary newspaper reports reveal the impression that MacDonald made on his audience. His voice, they record, was clear, musical and capable of a variety of expression and his manner conversational so that he spoke straight to the people's hearts, but above all it was the man's soul that captivated, so that one could not help loving him.

But the tour was not without its troubles. A serious fire broke out in Boston while they were there which destroyed the greater part of the city so that they had to be evacuated from Charles Street. Not infrequently bronchitis caught up with George leading to cancellation of some lectures. They both found travelling tiring. On one occasion the train in which they were travelling to Pittsburg was held up by a derailment and they were in the train for seventeen hours instead of the scheduled eleven, and that on the coldest night of the winter. Inevitably George was taken ill.

Their travels in the States were very extensive taking them from Boston to Chigaco, Ann Arbor near Detroit, New York, Cincinnati, Delaware, Ohio, Altoona, Pennsylvania, Buffalo, Milton Massachusetts and to Washington to stay with his old friends, the Russell Gurneys, Russell having recently accepted a diplomatic appointment. Consequently there was little time for sight-seeing. A visit to Niagara Falls described by Louisa to her daughter Lilia appears to have been the only official holiday excursion:

114

...Niagara was our greatest and only treat of the kind since we came. The standing on the top of the Terrapin Tower and feeling borne up and away from everything and seeing those mighty waves rolling and dashing beneath us brought the idea of infinity and majesty more intent upon me than anything in my life — anything material I mean, that ever I saw... I imagine that I knew more certainly than ever before what it would be to have a spiritual body and belong to creation — not merely to this little earth-bit of it..

Although ostensibly the main purpose of the tour was to improve his financial position, George MacDonald did not in fact make a fortune. Some of his lectures had to be cancelled because of ill health and for these cases the fees were not forthcoming, but George did not regard lecturing on literary subjects as the only reason for his presence in America. He saw it as an opportunity for preaching. In fact his fame as a preacher became even greater than his acclaim as a lecturer. It took a great toll of his strength and more often than not he refused any remuneration.

In the little University town of Ann Arbor other places of worship were closed so that all should have the chance of hearing George's eloquence. As his wife reported in a letter to Lilia 'he was inspired, speaking as if by the power of the spirit within him'. On another occasion he preached in New York. While there, they attended a concert given by the Jubilee Singers who were black. They sang of their experiences as slaves and George was greatly moved. Then they sang the Lord's Prayer which in Louisa's view was equal to any cathedral music. At the end of the performance someone turned down the gas-light and one of the singers called out 'all the same colour now'.

Above all George MacDonald valued the opportunities for new friendships which the American tour provided. The poet R.W. Gilder became a life-long friend and visited George and Louisa in Italy. He had a deeper insight than most into George's romantic and spiritual outlook and had a deep love for him as a man apart from his public image. He even called the MacDonalds Papa and Mama, and was a great favourite with Greville. Another good friend was the Revd George Bacon at whose Church in Orange Valley, New Jersey George MacDonald was invited to preach. Then there was Doctor

Bellows, a Unitarian Minister with whom George enjoyed exchanging views. Mark Twain too became a friend and they discussed at one time cooperation on a novel together so as to secure copyright on both sides of the Atlantic. But unfortunately the project never came off, due partly to difference in style and motive.

Wherever they went the MacDonalds were entertained with as much deference as royalty and this included Louisa whose graciousness, charm and unaffected delight in her husband's success, won all hearts. George could never have survived the eight month ordeal without Louisa's support, her determination to keep 'lion-hunters' at bay and her tender care for his bodily needs in which she never flagged even after hearing George lecture on Burns for the fortieth time.

Before they left America, George's admirers inaugurated a testimonial to compensate him for the loss of copyright on many pirated editions of his books published in America. It amounted to 1,500 dollars. He was asked to give a farewell lecture in New York and was also offered a church there, but in spite of being exceedingly touched by the kindness and goodwill he had been shown on all sides, he did not feel drawn to the idea of permanent residence in the States. It is significant perhaps, that in none of the books which he wrote after his return to England is there any reference to America. In May 1873 the MacDonalds sailed for home to a joyful re-union with their other ten children.

George's writing benefited from the few months it had been in abeyance and he returned with a renewed zest for literary work. He had been planning a novel with an Aberdeenshire background before he went to America and had indeed made a preliminary visit to Huntly with this in view shortly before his departure. In the autumn of 1873 he returned there accompanied by Louisa and two of the children, to explore more thoroughly Cullen on the north coast which under the name of Portlossie would be the setting for *Malcolm*. The chief characters in this novel such as Duncan Macphail, the blind piper and the young fisher lad Malcolm with those of the sequel in *The Marquis of Lossie*, are some of the most convincing in all his books and believed to be based on local personalities. *Malcolm* was eventually published in 1875.

About this time the second daughter Mary Josephine became engaged to Edward R. Hughes, a young artist, and nephew of the artist Arthur Hughes, illustrator of MacDonald's fairy tales. He was very good-looking, charming and hard-working, and it was generally considered a suitable match, but unfortunately Mary Josephine contracted tuberculosis after an attack of scarlet fever and this tragedy, together with the fact that her father's own health was far from satisfactory, led to the conclusion that the riverside home, The Retreat, was to blame and must be given up.

After moves to various temporary abodes such as Great Tangley Manor near Guildford, and a new house set in the midst of pines at Bournemouth whence George was able to visit his great friends the Cowper-Temples at Broadlands, Romsey, a decision was made that Mary must be taken to the Italian Riviera to seek a cure. MacDonald was too much involved at the time with the business of getting his latest novel, *Paul Faber, Surgeon* published to leave the country. So in Autumn 1877 in spite of great difficulty in raising enough for their travelling expenses, Louisa, Mary and three of the other children set off for Italy. They found at Nervi, near Genoa, in the Riviera di Levante, an inexpensive house to rent, Palazzo Cattaneo. George longed to join them but was detained by his business difficulties and another attack of pleurisy. His faith was sorely tested at this time with Mary's illness and his own insolvency but help as always was at hand in the shape of a gift of £200 from William Cowper Temple and a Civil pension of £100 a year from the Queen obtained through the influence of Princess Alice to whom he had been presented the previous year. On the strength of this George at last decided to join his wife and four children at Palazzo Cattaneo with the remainder of his family. It was set in orange groves, a vast cheerless church-like building with marble floors, stone stair-cases, iron balustrades and frescoed walls, hardly an ideal building to serve as a sanitorium but in George's eyes it was redeemed by affording a superb view of blue Mediterranean waters.

They were happy there that first Christmas of 1877 and George wrote a greeting in verse for his friends which has found its way into the Oxford Book of Victorian Verse:

> They all were looking for a King
> To slay their foes and lift them high:
> He came a little baby thing
> That made a woman cry.

> O Son of Man, to right my lot
> Nought but thy presence can avail;
> Yet on the road thy wheels are not,
> Nor on the sea thy sail!

> My how or when thou wilt not heed,
> But come down thine own secret stair,
> That thou mayst answer all my need —
> Yea, every by-gone prayer.

It was a message of reassurance to himself as much as to his friends. At a time when his fortunes were at a low ebb he had been tempted, as he expressed it himself to his wife, by the Apollyon of unbelief, God had of his goodness unexpectedly provided him with the wherewithal to be re-united with his family.

But greater trials awaited the MacDonald family. Mary Josephine's health did not improve through the Italian winter and on April 27th, 1878 she died. Edward (Ted) Hughes was at her death bed. They had been engaged for four years. George and Louisa suffered more intensely over the loss than they had ever done before. Although George at least outwardly and in answer to letters of sympathy was able to philosophise about death and look forward to a reunion with his child in the hereafter, Louisa was heart-broken and found at first no consolation in Christian beliefs. Without her beloved Mary to tend, she felt perhaps, full of regret that they had been able to do so little to effect a cure. She may have realised with some bitterness that the near poverty line on which the family had often, owing to her husband's tender conscience, subsisted, must have contributed to the breakdown in Mary's health. In a poem written for his wife's birthday in 1878 George MacDonald shows that he appreciates the doubt and agony through which she is passing, and does not force upon her the 'pleasant fancies of a half-held creed' but invites her instead to step out with him to find Mary's new abode 'to climb the stair where death is one wide landing to the rooms above'.

When the lease of Palazzo Cattaneo expired, the family moved for a year to the Villa Barratta at nearby Porto Fino, a delightfully situated house overlooking the bay near Rapallo, east of Genoa. As Greville recalls, the children enjoyed swimming and boating in the sea which was on their doorstep.

The cost of living was cheap in comparison with Britain so they decided to remain in Italy for a while. In the meantime George's writing was progressing well. *Paul Faber* was already near publication and *Sir Gibbie*, a beautiful Scottish pastoral was appearing in serial form.

But less than a year after Mary Josephine's death they lost another very dear child. This time it was the fifteen year old Maurice, the most promising of all their boys – intelligent, sensitive and highly imaginative. He contracted pneumonia and died after only eighteen days' illness. Because the MacDonalds were not Catholics, Maurice was buried in unconsecrated ground in a cemetery on a rocky promontory at Porto Fino overlooking the sea and washed by the waves when the sea is stormy. After so much sadness caused by the loss of two children George and Louisa were glad to welcome the Watson Gilders and their little boy for a visit.

This time of testing which George MacDonald had undergone bore triumphant fruit in his 'Book of Strife' or 'The Diary of an Old Soul'. It is written in Rime Royal, provides one stanza for each day of the year and reveals the steadfast faith in life after death which his experiences had built up in him. Like Donal Grant he faces the fact that there can be no intellectual proof of continuing life as is comparable with our knowledge of the phenomenon of physical death, yet he knows that God is the beginning and end of all things and that faith is confirmed in the doing and accepting of His will. The *Diary of an Old Soul* was published privately in 1880.

George and Louisa were resolved to continue to spend the winters in Italy but it would be necessary to find a more permanent home as renting property was unsettling and precarious. Such a project would, however, need funds for the purchase of a house, for transporting their effects and also the family, between the two countries, as summers would still be spent in England. Louisa took upon herself most of the fund-raising by organizing the family in productions of play sometimes by Shakespeare, but chiefly *The Pilgrim's Progress*. It was in this that the MacDonalds gave their best and most memorable performance with Lilia as Christiana and George himself as Greatheart. He was indeed so popular in the part and made such a deeply spiritual impact on the audience that he was affectionately called by his friends Mr Greatheart. Staging the play made heavy demands on the whole family for they provided all their own props and costumes, painted the scenery and were responsible for their own publicity. Some friends and acquaintances disapproved of their acting on the grounds that they were cheapening themselves and the sacred nature of Bunyan's allegory by presenting it commercially, but others realised that it would speak for itself by being presented so reverently and with such sincerity and could indeed do a tremendous amount of good.

The MacDonalds needed the money not only to provide for their own family but Louisa had in 1881 added to the household a woman who had been deserted by a French husband, and her two little girls. They had in addition already given a home to a little orphan boy while they were at The Retreat. With funds raised from theatrical productions added to a testimonial subscribed to by various friends and well-wishers which included Princess Alice of Hesse, the Earl and Countess of Ducie, the Cowper-Temples, Russell Gurneys and many other of their personal friends, enough money was acquired to purchase the freehold of land at Bordighera in the Italian Riviera, twenty miles from Nice and to build a house there planned by George MacDonald himself. It was called Casai Coraggio and was larger than was really needed, but its generously proportioned rooms provided opportunities for entertaining which formed such an important feature of the MacDonald family life. Like most of the architecture in that part of Italy it was baroque in style. The largest room which served as George's study measured fifty-two by twenty-six feet and housed a two manual pipe organ. Meals were eaten here and it was used for social gatherings, entertainments, lectures and religious meetings. MacDonald continued lectures on literary subjects, 'At Homes' were held and Nativity Tableaux presented at Christmas, as well, of course, as performances of *The Pilgrim's Progress*. There was quite a large population of English residents at Bordighera at that time and a well developed social life in which the MacDonalds gladly joined. Casai Coraggio was tastefully, even Bohemianly furnished and decorated, much of the work being done by the family themselves. George was able to put into practice some of the ideas he had absorbed on architecture from Ruskin and also to indulge his penchant for bright colours. Lilia wrote to a friend Jane Cobden describing the work of redecoration. 'We are all steeped to our elbows in black paint and coloured stains for wood. Mamma and Grace are doing the walls of Mamma's little sitting-room, a dull red with eucalyptus leaves all over it'.

Although most of their furniture had not arrived from England, by Christmas 1880 the family had moved in and they were already inviting visitors to stay who made the best of the improvised seats which the MacDonald girls were constructing. Christmas was celebrated with carol singing and a Christmas tree as was their wont, the Italian children mingling with their personal friends. Later a concert was given to raise funds for the local Catholic Church, for George was nothing if not ecumenically minded. Poetry readings alternated with less sedate functions such as a bonfire to which friends were invited to bring their own fuel in the shape of old clothes and unwanted papers. An invitation was composed in humorous verse. The bonfire was followed by dancing. No matter what the function, the guests felt welcomed and part of the family. A neighbour Lord Mount-Temple was able to recall in his 'Memorials' that, 'That house, Coraggio, is the very heart of Bordighera, the rich core of it, always raying out to all around, and gathering them to itself'.

It was not only the house to which George felt deeply attached but also its delightful setting. An exile from Scotland for so many years, he adopted Italy as his second home. He loved the bright blue Italian skies, the distant views of the snow-capped Maritime Alps, the dark green olive groves climbing up the hillsides, the orangeries and gardens blossoming with mimosa at Christmas time, and the masses of magenta-coloured bouganvillea even in January. He enjoyed walking to little hill-top villages with their narrow winding streets and houses built in terraces on either side approached by steep stone staircases; and casting their protective shadow over all the ancient turreted churches. The mild climate in the Riviera di Ponente protected as it is from the northern winds by the mountains, was beneficial to his health. He delighted in the semi-tropical vegetation and the wealth of flowers which are grown westward along the coast towards Monte Carlo and abundance of date palms from which, even to this day, palm branches are supplied to Churches all over Italy for the ceremonies on Palm Sunday as well as for the Jewish Feast of Tabernacles.

George's love for the Italian countryside finds expression in the one book which he wrote with an Italian background, *A Rough Shaking*, published in 1890. It also recreates one of the most terrifying experiences of their lives: the earthquake of 1887. In the book it is most vividly described by the fictional Clare Skymer whose mother was killed in the disaster

'all at once the whole bulk of the huge building [the Church in which the villagers had taken refuge] began to shudder and went on shuddering like the skin of a horse determined to get rid of a gad-fly − the tiles on the roof began to clatter like so many castanets in the hands of giants and the ground to wriggle and heave. Down came plaster. Some rushed out into the square, then came a roaring crash and a huge rumbling and through which rose a multitudinous shriek of terror, agony, a number of men and women issued as if shot from a catapult, then no more, the roof had fallen on the rest. The shaking ceased utterly. Of what had taken place there was no sign on the earth, no sign in the blue sun-glorious heaven, only in the air there was a cloud of dust... and from it issued a ghostly cry mingled with shrieks, groans and articulate appeals for help'.

The earthquake took place early in the morning of February 23rd, 1887 and lasted for about five hours. Casa Coraggio being of stouter construction suffered less damage than the humbler dwellings of most of the population in the area, sustaining only cracked plaster in ceilings and an avalanche of broken china, books and papers. But the tower built into the house which was made of stucco, not stone as was the rest of the house, had to be demolished as unsafe. The MacDonald family, as one might have expected, set about relieving the sufferings of any victims within their reach, providing meals for those whose kitchens had been destroyed and shelter to a homeless family in the large room used for lectures and entertainments. George MacDonald's reaction was also predictable. He took the disaster literally as an act of God. 'That shock', he wrote to his friend Carey Davies, 'was worth having lived to know what power may be. You knew it must be none other than God. No lesser power could hold the earth like that as if it were a very little thing, and shake you as if your big house were a dolls' fly'.

Long term relief measures included sewing parties to make clothes for those who had lost everything in the quake. Many people camped out under the olive trees as the tremors continued, though less severe, for about a fortnight. Throughout most of the period George continued to write, reassuring their friends and neighbours by his serenity in the midst of chaos.

During the decade 1880 to 1890 the MacDonald family had begun to scatter. In 1881 Grace had married the English Chaplain at Bordighera, Kingsbury Jameson and they had one child Octavia to whom Louisa was devoted. But she died at the age of nine, predeceased by her mother in 1884. Both died of tubercular infection. Greville had qualified as a doctor and had a practice in Harley Street. Ranald had obtained a good history degree at Oxford and had taken up school-mastering. He married in 1888 and went to the U.S.A. where his wife died two years later. Lilia, the eldest was one of the most strong-minded of all the children. Throughout the changes and chances of their family life she had had the responsibility of providing stability for the younger children. She was sensitive to their needs and also had an insight into her father's spirituality and her mother's reverence for it. But she felt she had her own contribution to make through her gift for acting and took the part of Christiana in *The Pilgrim's Progress* with the utmost seriousness. When the man to whom she became engaged tried to persuade her to give up acting as a profession unworthy of a woman, she refused to do so and reluctantly broke off the engagement. This unshakeable loyalty to what she believed to be her duty, was evident in all Lilia's actions. When her brother Ranald was left a widower in 1890 she went to Ashville, North Carolina, to keep house for him in the boys' school of which he was Headmaster, but a year later hearing that a great friend who had wintered with them in Italy was seriously ill with tuberculosis, she returned home to nurse her and contracted the disease herself. The MacDonald family was based at Stoke Rectory, Billericay during the summer of 1891. While Louisa was nursing Lilia and anxiously looking for some sign of improvement, George was on his last lecture tour. It took him among other places to Huntly, where he preached in the Presbyterian Church and met old friends. With his cousin James who had now taken over the farm, he revisited the scenes of his childhood and found the country more beautiful than ever. It was a nostalgic visit. He must have felt like Robert Falconer when he returned to Rothieden after many years, to search for Shargar's mother.

> 'He walked through the odours of grass and of clover and of the yellow flowers on the old earth walls that divided the fields.... sweet scents which, mingling with the smell of the earth itself reach the founts of memory sooner than ever words or tones — down to the river that flowed scarcely murmuring from its far off birthplace in the peaty hills. He crossed the footbridge and turned into the bleachfield. Its houses were desolate for that trade too had died away. The machinery stood rotting and rusting. The wheel gave no answering motion to the flow of the water that glided beneath it. The thundering beatles were still.... The canal, the delight of his childhood was nearly choked with weeds.... He climbed to the place where he had once lain.... hearing the voice of nature that whispered God in his ears and there he threw himself down once more. All the old things, the old ways, the old glories of childhood — were they gone? There is no past with Him. An eternal present. His history was taken up into God; it had not vanished; his life was hid with Christ in God'.

Lilia did not recover and the family returned in haste to Bordighera in October while it was still possible for her to travel. George remained behind to finish his lecture tour and also had the sad task of saying a last farewell to his friend William Matheson. Matheson had been in love with Lilia for several years, but had never declared his love as he considered himself too old for her. As it was he predeaceased her by one day, for George MacDonald's 'little white lily' died on November 22nd 1891 at the age of thirty-nine. Christiana had for the last time crossed the river to the Celestial City. She died in the arms of Mr Greatheart her father.

Once again Louisa was full of reproaches for herself and her husband. She realised the suffering they had both unwittingly inflicted on their children. 'Knowing all I do now', she wrote to her husband, 'of what unintentional agonies we have made our children suffer all the while having a heart full of love and intended good will to them, I could not dare of my own choice have over again such a lovely family as was given to us to rear and teach and guide'.

Sunset

The last decade of the old century was full of the sadness of farewells, not that George MacDonald would admit to grieving at his friends' departure into a fuller life. When he heard of the death of Tennyson in 1892 whose poetry in general he greatly admired and 'In Memoriam' in particular, he wrote to his secretary, W. Carey Davies, 'I do not mourn much for any of the dead. God be with us here and there – that is all'. One of the last letters he wrote was to Carey Davies' wife on hearing of her husband's sudden death at the comparatively early age of fifty-five in 1898. It came as a great shock to him and affected him mentally so that he felt he was losing his grip. Although his faith in a life after death never failed, he believed his own time was drawing nearer and it sapped his creative energy. But at the beginning of the decade he was still writing powerfully. Some of his best books belong to this period, such as *There and Back* published in 1891 and *Lilith* in 1895.

Although written so much later than *Phantastes*, *Lilith* is in the nature of a companion volume. In it MacDonald gets to grips with the nature and meaning of death, clothing it, because death is incomprehensible in abstract terms to those who can have no first hand experience of it, in strangely concrete imagery. *Lilith* in rabbinical literature was once the wife of Adam, but when she bore him a child, she was puffed up with her own importance and challenged God. When Adam refused to worship her she made an alliance with the evil one called The Shadow and took the form of a vampire stalking the world and lying in wait to ensnare the souls of 'the little ones'. The revelation of what death means and the various processes through which a soul must pass on its way to blessedness is given to a man called Vane by a talking Raven and his wife who turn out to be Adam and Eve. In the cemetery to which the Raven takes Vane, the temperature is excruciatingly cold and there the dead in happy acceptance of sleep are purified of all evil and await the renewal of their youth and the restoration of their innocence. As each sin which blemishes the soul is gradually healed, so the perfection of its beauty is recovered.

By his most extraordinarily graphic, yet bizarre imagery, George MacDonald is preaching a sermon on the resurrection of the dead. Yet at the same time he warns his readers that Hell does exist even though it cannot have the last word, good being stronger than evil. Death is a state in which evil must be shown in its true colours and finally rejected by the human soul. At the beginning of the book Vane did not want to surrender himself to death when the Raven showed him the couch in the cemetery which was awaiting him, but in the end he realised that only by accepting it, could victory over evil be won. He had to learn the full horror of wickedness before he would be prepared to seek his tomb. He is therefore introduced to scenes of unimaginable horror, such as the dance of the skeletons.

MacDonald's view of death made a great impression on C.S. Lewis. In *The Great Divorce* in which he imagines that souls may make excursions from Hell to Heaven with the option of remaining there, Lewis makes it plain that the dead only attain substance and reality for their resurrection bodies in so far as they surrender their earthly and worldly ambitions and acknowledge the existence of a spiritual fourth dimension to their lives. This was the lesson that Vane had also to learn from the Raven when that extraordinary bird told him to remove an ancient volume fixed on a shelf of dummy books. It leads him into a world of new dimensions where he is no longer bound by time and space and one in which it is possible to have a true vision of what is good and therefore beautiful, and what is evil and consequently ugly.

In his dream Vane eventually fought with Lilith who was disguised as a spotted leopard and was mortally wounded and laid on the couch prepared for him in the cemetery, but before he could experience death and subsequently record it, he awoke from his dream and returned to earth by way of the library through which he had come. He resumed his mortal life a changed man for he had glimpsed a vision of the truth inspired by faith.

C.S. Lewis describes a similar experience in *The Great Divorce* when with George MacDonald as his guide he is privileged to see the difference between the reality of heaven and the ghostly world of hell. But the interview ends with a warning from his mentor that what he has seen must not be taken as an exact picture of heaven. It is only a dream.

Louisa MacDonald's health began to fail after Lilia's death. George took her to Switzerland in the summer of 1892 with the hope of reviving her body, mind and spirit, but she refused to give in to her weakness and once back in Bordighera for the winter she continued to play the organ at the English Church.

George in the meantime was busy preparing for publication a collected volume of his poems. He did a certain amount of revision on them though he was not really convinced that he could improve them. The mass of his novels show what a perfectionist he was in his choice of words and turn of phrase, altering and re-writing a passage again and again, but with his poetry he felt that his original idea, though obscure perhaps to his reader, could not be easily revised and its inspiration recaptured.

The volume of poems was issued in 1893 and in the same year a collection of MacDonald's essays on literary subjects which had formed the basis of his lectures, entitled *A Dish of Orts* was published. From the standpoint of literary criticism they were not widely acclaimed even by his contemporaries and Greville himself admitted that his father was 'never what mere schoolmen consider a first-rate academic critic, perhaps just because he was so very much more'. Yet for psychological interpretation and spiritual insight, especially with regard to Shakespearian characters such as Hamlet, Macbeth and King Lear, some of his essays are most illuminating. Some of the lectures contained in the volume had been delivered in America where as Louisa MacDonald reports in letters to her family they were enthusiastically received. Of his lecture on *Macbeth* she reports that he sent his audience into 'cold shivers' over the Ghost and sleep walking scenes, and Greville who was present at his father's lecture on Burns records that 'the public discovered one aspect of his genius — his power of inspired, uplifting criticism in no way spoiled by his just facing of facts. Through his wise and weighty poetic and passionate words, without notes or help other than a volume of Burns' works, he set the man before them, the lover, the romantic ploughman, the poet in true portraiture while his sins and shortcomings were fully accredited to him.... It was new to an American audience to hear such eloquence unbuttressed by academic elocution'.

These publications together with his last novels brought him increasingly into the public eye. Although fans and sight-seers became more troublesome George always refused to be interviewed. He did not wish to be recognized by his public image but to be remembered for the message which by his writing he sought to convey.

By 1894 the MacDonalds were back in Italy, and now without the pressure of constant writing George was able to enjoy the delights of the Riviera, undertaking expeditions to Cape Montola on the borders of Monaco and the wooded heights of San Romolo over two thousand feet up above San Remo. He even ventured further afield, visiting friends as far away as Pisa and Florence. He retained the same childlike wonder and appreciation of natural beauty which had characterised his childhood. But he felt his mental powers were declining and he was suffering from eczema which tortured him at night and deprived him of sleep, although he kept his brain as active as possible by studying Spanish and Dutch.

One of the last letters he wrote was to Carey Davies' wife on hearing of her husband's sudden death.

Dear Mrs Davies

...I have been indeed unable to think, and still more to know what I was thinking. Indeed I feel sometimes as if I were about to lose all power of thought. But when I find Carey again, he will help to set me right. Ah you will be glad when you go to him, and find him all right and well and happy! Surely our Lord meant no less for us! He is in joy and peace with him.

I am drawing nearer to the time I shall have to go. I do not think it will be just yet, and it is a good thing we should not know when the call will come but may He give me what readiness he pleases. I should like to be as ready as your husband. I do not think I can ever be more ready than he.

Write to me again although I do not deserve it...

With the gradual failing health of their parents which made travel to Italy increasingly difficult, the MacDonald children were anxious to provide a more secure and comfortable home for them. Their son Robert Falconer who had trained as an architect, designed a house for them at Haslemere called St George's Wood and there they came to live. Here too they celebrated their golden wedding in 1901. But sadly it was not to be their home for long as Louisa was suffering from an incurable disease, probably cancer, and a cloud of partial unknowing seems to have descended upon George's mind. When Louisa died in 1902 he appeared quite bewildered like a dog who has lost his master. Although bereft of speech, he was patiently resigned with his gaze fixed upon the far distances. Greville describes the characteristic state of his father during these final months: 'He spent much of his time in bed. But whether there or sitting dressed, he was always waiting, always beautiful to behold, in spite of the cloud upon the snow-clad mountain. If anyone came to the door for entry, he would turn and look with a moment's quiet expectation, and seeing it was not my mother, would sigh deeply and begin his waiting again. He was keeping the long vigil till she came for him'. His release came on September 18th, 1905.

> I lie like unhatched bird upfolded dumb
> While all the air is trembling with the hum
> Of songs and beating hearts and whirring wings
> That call my slumbering life to wake to happy things.
> My waking life is hid with Christ in God
> Where all is true and potent — fact divine....
> I will not heed the thing that doth but seem
> I will be quiet as lark upon the sod.
> God's will, the seed shall rest in me the pod.

> Diary of an Old Soul

George MacDonald died at Ashstead in Surrey where he had been devotedly cared for by his youngest daughter Winifred Louisa

Troup. After cremation at Woking his ashes were conveyed to Bordighera and buried beside the body of his wife amid the fragrant orange groves and under the bright Italian Skies which they both had loved so well.

Epilogue

If one's assessment of George MacDonald's religious views is based mainly on the events of his life, a somewhat negative picture will be obtained. So much has been written about his protest, made chiefly in the novels, against the seemingly uncharitable and unchristian doctrines of Calvinism, his condemnation of formalism and hypocrisy in the clergy, their sermons and their worship, that it is reasonable to wonder to what denomination if any he did in his heart of hearts subscribe. In answer to this one cannot be categorical. It seems clear that he had already in his youth renounced the tenets of orthodox Calvinism and embraced the more liberal views of some congregationalists, but when this also proved too restricting to his tender-hearted approach to his fellow men as well as to his understanding of the just and loving Fatherhood of God, he remained 'out on a limb' for a time, largely deprived of preaching the gospel of love in which he so passionately believed, until in his late forties he met the great and holy F.D. Maurice. Under his guidance and impressed by his example, yet of his own volition, George MacDonald became a confirmed member of the Church of England. Clearly Anglican teaching most closely coincided with his own beliefs at that time.

Intellectual honesty, however, made it impossible for him to subscribe unconditionally to the Thirty-nine Articles and this deterred him from seeking Anglican Orders. Throughout his life it was necessary for him to reserve the right to question and face up to doubt as the 'hammer that breaks the windows clouded with human fancies and lets in the pure light'. Doubts he believed, are the messengers of the living one to the honest. They are the first knock at the door of things that are not yet, but have to be understood. Doubt must precede every deeper assurance.

MacDonald did not accept a fundamentalist view of the Bible. It is not the word that is inspired, else he maintained, it would be better written but as in every human activity, he believed, God helped the compilers to use their commonsense and intellectual powers to write what they believed to be true. George MacDonald valued the Scriptures as giving an account of the life of Jesus, but it is his own conscience or Christ dwelling in him that was his chief guide in living. For he believed above all in the immanence of God at the heart of all creation: 'Man is a creek into which the infinite ocean of life ebbs and flows. God is present in all beauty, his tenderness in all fatherhood, in *The Diary of an Old Soul* he expressed this thought which some have taken as an indication of his leanings towards the Roman Catholic Church and the doctrine of Transubstantiation:

> ...from every clod
> Into thy foot-print flows the indwelling wine,
> And in my daily bread, keen-eyed I greet
> Its being's heart, the very body of God.

But the freedom of thought which an immanent God bestowed upon him would have made it impossible for him to accept unquestioningly the restrictions and disciplines of such a creed. He had a firm belief in the right of an individual to make his own unique response to the will of God as expressed through his own conscience. This did not lead to laxity and misguided wishful thinking and self-deception. To George MacDonald God's love was inexorable and made the highest demands, 'for our God is a consuming fire and all that is not of love's kind must be destroyed'. 'There is no refuge from the love of God, that love will for very love insist upon the uttermost farthing'.

This love MacDonald perceived to be at work in creation which he saw as an on-going process, gradual but sure and finally to be consummated through the Incarnation, Redemption and Resurrection of Christ. The new creation is to include animals too. They are waiting for their adoption when they will be brought into a peaceful relationship with man when the latter has been redeemed.

MacDonald's passionate love of animals and especially of horses had its origin in this vision of the partnership which should exist between the human and bestial creation. 'He [God] knows His horses and dogs as we cannot know them because we are not yet pure sons of God. When through our sonship, as Paul teaches, the redemption of our lower brothers and sisters shall have come, then we shall understand each other better. But now the Lord of Life has to look on at the wilful torture of multitudes of His creatures. It must be that offences come but woe unto that man by whom they come!' (*Unspoken Sermons*, 3rd Series).

The many horses in his novels are living portraits of his own experience of this most noble of creatures, beginning with Missy the white pony of his childhood and progressing to Memnon the magnificent Arab, Skymer's almost human horse in *A Rough Shaking* whom his master sent on his own to deliver messages. There are delightful sketches of dogs too — one was called Tadpole because he had the hugest tail, while his legs were not visible without being looked for — yet he was the cleverest of all because he inherited the best from each of his assorted ancestors! George believed in their immortality; perhaps as with all who suffer heartbreak at the loss of their pets it was partly wishful thinking, a hope having its origin in neither scientific or religious thought; but it was more than that. His belief was based on his realisation that the nature of animals, indeed their very existence, had its origin in the creative love of God whose work is to preserve not to destroy. Through the lips of Peter Simon, Cosmo's schoolmaster in *Castle Warlock*, George MacDonald delivered the same message of hope regarding his pupil's mare Linty who was very old and seriously ill: 'That a thing can love and be loved is the same as saying it is immortal, for God is love and whatever partakes of the essence of God cannot die'. In 1870 MacDonald wrote to a friend on hearing that he had recently lost his dear dog Dash, 'I trust for him it is only a fresh finding of himself — that delicate long nose of his was not given him for only such a few years as you have known him'.

Above all George believed in the resurrection of man's body and everlasting life.

I love you my sweet children who are gone
Into another mansion, but I know
I love you not as I shall love you yet.

He looks forward to a reunion with his dead son Maurice

Twilight of the transfiguration — joy,
Gleam-faced pure-eyed, strong-willed high-hearted boy!
Hardly thy life clear forth of heaven was sent
Ere it broke out into a smile and went.
So swift thy growth, so true thy goalward bent
Thou, child and sage inextricably blent
Must surely one day come to teach thy father in some heavenly tent'

And of Mary Josephine, his 'blackbird', he writes

Again I shall behold the daughter true;
The hour shall come when I shall hold thee fast
In God's name, loving thee all through and through,
Somewhere in his grand thought this waits for us.

These lines contemplating the afterlife are taken from *Diary of an Old Soul.*

Because George MacDonald believed in God as a loving father-creator, infinitely more loving and more understanding than the best of earthly fathers, he could not accept that He could predestine any to eternal loss. This does not mean that he believed in a wholesale influx of humanity into heaven and the bliss of eternal life. He believed in the reality of hell but saw it as a training school or hospital for sin-sick souls where they could be healed and helped to see reality as they had never seen it on earth. The more a person can be helped to make the right choices in this life, the better chance he will have of finding his place in heaven. This point MacDonald makes most poignantly and solemnly in *Lilith* where Vane is taken by the Raven to visit the mortuary in Adam and Eve's house and finds the dead sleeping while they await their final purification and ultimately joyful resurrection.

MacDonald's belief in the omnipotence of God made it difficult for him to accept the possibility that some souls might be lost. Would not such a contingency amount to failure on God's part? Yet he realised that the very nature of love is its spontaneity and freedom. Love cannot be forced and if a man refuses to respond of his own free-will even Love itself cannot force that soul's response and acceptance of salvation. Such intransigence amounts in the end to what Jesus calls a sin against the Holy Ghost which cannot be forgiven for it loves darkness rather than light and persists in calling evil good and vice versa. Consequently it was a matter of the greatest urgency to MacDonald that by prayer, example and acts of Christ-like love, everyone, as far as possible, should be enabled to experience the love of God in this world and be given an opportunity to respond to it. If it sometimes seems that nothing short of a miracle could bring this about, MacDonald would say that he believed in the miracles of Jesus as 'the ordinary works of his Father wrought small and swift that we might take them in'. To him they are the epitome of God's processes in nature speeded up in response to man's faith. The miracle at Cana for example, when he multiplied the wine is no more grand and beautiful than the work of the Father which he represented 'in making corn to grow in the valleys and grapes to drink the sunlight on the hill-sides of the world'.

MacDonald published in 1870 a whole series of sermons on the subject of miracles and dedicated them to F.D. Maurice. Writing three quarters of a century later, C.S. Lewis in a book with the same title, *The Miracles of Our Lord* interpreted the miracle at Cana in a similar way. God he says, in Jesus, is short-circuiting a process in which he is always involved in the cycle of nature, producing the harvests of the world. Both writers deal thoroughly with every type of miracle recorded in the Gospels whether concerned with nature or human nature, but above all they deal with those which concern the life of Christ himself − the Incarnation, Transfiguration and Resurrection. To George MacDonald the Resurrection is not a mere promise of immortality to man which can be backed up in man's wishful thinking or by recourse to a spiritualistic medium in contact with some ghostly world. He regarded the evangelists' accounts of the appearances as an assurance of a resurrection body of a corporeal nature but with added powers bestowed upon Christ by the in-dwelling presence of the spirit of his Father, and promised to man. 'I think of death as the first pulse of the new strength shaking itself free from the old mouldy remnants of earth garments, that it may begin in freedom the new life that grows out of the old. The caterpillar dies into the butterfly'.

As far as George MacDonald was concerned one might suppose that he would have been glad to think that the resurrection of the body to which he so ardently looked forward, might have been of a less corporeal nature. Judging from the way he conducted himself in public and ordered his life, lecturing and preaching at home and abroad, and forcing himself to write long novels, it must have been difficult for the public to realise how intensely he suffered physically from almost constant ill-health, chronic bronchitis, asthma and headaches, and the threat of lung disease as well as in latter years from a skin complaint and insomnia. Poverty and the threat of insolvency were never far from the door. What was it that kept him outwardly cheerful and inwardly resigned to the will of God? It was undoubtedly the strength which he derived from prayer, a practice which he never gave up in spite of weariness. We are given a glimpse of the problem in his *Diary of an Old Soul* which, significantly, was given the alternative title *A Book of Strife*.

> Some times, hard-trying, it seems I cannot pray
> For doubts and pain and anger and all strife.
> Yet some poor half-fledged prayer-bird from the nest
> May fall, flit, perch − crouch in the bowery breast
> Of the large nation-healing tree of life.
> Moveless there sit through all the burning day
> And on my heart at night a fresh leaf cooling lay.
> ...my harvest withers. Health, my means to live −
> All things seem rushing straight into the dark.
> But the dark still is God.

Paradoxically perhaps, it was in his hour of greatest trials that his life made most impact on the world around him. In times of disappointment, failure and poverty his faith shone out triumphantly. He had a child-like faith which refused to accept defeat or doubt the loving Fatherhood of God watching over the ups and downs of his life however desperate they might be. This dated back, in all probability, to happy recollections of parental tenderness at home and he remembered that a bitter pill in the end makes for health and happiness, or as Paul Faber put it, 'I think when the sun rises upon them, some people will be surprised to find how far they have got in the dark'.

But George MacDonald's innocence found expression in other ways and it was probably this which endeared him to his family and friends and through his writing to his readers. To the child's trustfulness was added great joy in living. George loved life and all it had to offer — the beauty of the countryside and all living creatures. He enjoyed good food, bright colours and romantic clothes. He took a delight in his appearance and liked to have beautiful things around him in his home. Travel was an unending source of interest to him and nearly to the end of his life he was keen to visit new places and meet new people. It was all part of the wonderful world which God had created for men to preserve and enjoy.

George's own childlike simplicity gave him a sense of affinity with and reverence for all children. He believed in them as mirroring, before the image could be defaced, the beauty of holiness, with which they had come from their home in heaven. His reverence for children is reflected in his writing. Though idealised and bearing what some might consider to be an impossible yet unmistakable likeness to Christ, his portrait of the little dumb orphan baronet, Sir Gibbie, is one of the most moving and poignantly beautiful in the English language. Gibbie holds our attention and draws us to him with bands of compassionate love because his goodness is so attractive. He restores our belief in human nature and makes us long to identify with his innocence, trust and self-giving love of his persecutors. MacDonald's children are always convincing, delightful and sympathetically, not sentimentally, drawn.

George's love of children was not a mere fiction. He was genuinely devoted to his own and the greatest sorrow of his life and the most severe test of his faith in God's providence was caused by the untimely death of three of them. By to-day's standards the MacDonalds could perhaps be accused of negligence with regard to their children's schooling for none of them, except the boys in their teens, appear to have attended school or been given a formal education; but George (and no doubt Louisa was in agreement in the matter as a great deal of the children's education devolved upon her) believed in the natural development of a child's mind and character through the influence of environment, example and social intercourse. Like Peter Simon, Cosmos' tutor in *Castle Warlock*, George MacDonald judged it 'an imperative duty to leave room for his pupil to grow after the fashion in which he was made', and he believed 'that what a boy does by himself is of far greater import than what he does with any master'.

The MacDonald children were introduced, as far as their parents were able to provide, to all that was lovely and of good report, and they had ever before them the ideal of their father's transparent goodness and their mother's devoted care.

There was, however, an aspect of their upbringing upon which George was uncompromising and typical of the stern Victorian parent. He demanded and apparently received obedience from his children. But the discipline was exercised not in anger or displeasure but with the same loving wisdom which he had experienced in his relationship with his own father. Yet despite the dominant impression of a kind and loving father which Greville confirms in his biography of his parents, MacDonald's son is not without reservations. In *Reminiscences of a Specialist*, published in 1932, he gives voice to certain grievances:

> 'I doubt if I should question his theory of education except that it makes me look upon my father with some fear. He stood for the inexorable. So that when appeal to an undeveloped moral sense failed, corporal punishment, sometimes severe, was inevitable. It compelled submission, but never made me repentant. Certainly it did not encourage my brains. But worse, it made an over-sensitive child craving for love, so truly afraid of his father that more than once I lied to him'.

Another less attractive feature of his father emerges in a bias towards girls who were regarded as 'far above boys in goodness'. Greville reports that his sisters were never punished, that the MacDonalds' friendship with certain feminists of the day instilled in him a 'deep impression' in which 'the power of suggestion, though not yet formulated, thoroughly convinced me of my sex's inferiority'. This unfairness, coupled with MacDonald's painful and demoralizing attempts to explain Vergil and Euclid to his slow-learning son point to obvious faults in his character. But it is worth repeating that Greville's verdict on his father is generally favourable and indeed usually full of praise.

George's writing reveals little about his ideas of education with one exception. *The Vicar's Daughter* actually contains a list of precepts on how to bring up children which we may assume reflects the views of the author himself although not always realised in practice. They are too numerous to be quoted in full but they can be summarised as based on the principle of respect for the child's personality and rights as an individual. They include administering correction without sarcasm, ridicule or suspicion that the child is not speaking the truth and he should never be black-mailed into submission by threats of a religious nature. This is interesting as surely no father would be more likely to be tempted in this direction than George MacDonald himself. Above all discipline should be tempered with tolerance and children allowed to quarrel among themselves sometimes 'to clear the air', to make a lot of noise if they want to, and their complaints should always be listened to sympathetically.

In his own lifetime George MacDonald was revered as a poet, a novelist and a teacher whose spirituality and sheer goodness shone from his face as he lectured extempore to willing hearers, and from the pages of his books. But he was at heart a preacher. He wrote many sermons, most of which were never preached, and probably seldom read except by theologians, yet this does not matter, for his teaching shines clear in all his writings. It is incarnate in the flesh and blood of his characters. They speak the truth with simple directness and lift our gaze to the fullness of life which lies beyond the grave.

It was this directness and sureness of vision, the ability which young Diamond had in *At the Back of the North Wind* 'to look through the look of things' which appealed to C.S. Lewis and later inspired him to create his own 'other' world, where truth uncompromising and complete alone is the embodiment of reality.

'A poet,' North Wind told Diamond, 'is one who is glad of something and tries to make others glad of it too'. MacDonald was a poet and he made C.S. Lewis glad. He surprised him by joy with the gladness of finding God alive and at the centre of the Universe. We too can share that joy by reading George MacDonald's books and meeting him (as his son Greville writes) 'marching through the pages with bagpipes and bonnet and broadsword, making young and old alike feel a heroic joy in the eternal fight'.

BIBLIOGRAPHY
Works by George MacDonald, Primary Sources

FANTASIES
Phantastes, a Faerie Romance for Men and Women   1858
Lilith, a Romance   1895

NOVELS
David Elginbrod   1863
Adela Cathcart   1864
The Portent   1864
Alec Forbes of Howglen   1865
Annals of a Quiet Neighbourhood   1867
Robert Falconer   1868
The Seaboard Parish   1868
Ranald Bannerman's Boyhood   1871
The Vicar's Daughter   1872
Wilfred Cumbermede   1872
Gutta Percha Willie, The Working Genius   1873
Malcolm   1875
Thomas Wingfold, Curate   1876
St George, St Michael   1876
The Marquis of Lossie   1877
Sir Gibbie   1879
Paul Faber, Surgeon   1879
Mary Marston   1881
Gifts of the Christchild   1882
Castle Warlock   1882
Weighed and Wanting   1882
Donald Grant   1883
What's Mine's Mine   1886
Home Again   1887
The Elect Lady   1888
A Rough Shaking, a Tale   1890
There and Back   1891
Heather and Snow   1893
Salted with Fire, a Tale   1897
The World of George MacDonald
Selections from his fiction edited by Rolland Hein

STORIES FOR CHILDREN
★ Dealing with The Faeries 1867
   At The Back of The North Wind 1871
   The Princess and the Goblin 1872
   The Princess and the Curdie 1883
   The Light Princess and other Fairy Stories 1890
   The Lost Princess 1895
★ This first appeared in the novel *Adela Cathcart* 1864

THEOLOGICAL WORKS
Unspoken Sermons
       1st Series 1867
       2nd Series 1885
       3rd Series 1889
Miracles of Our Lord 1870
The Hope of the Gospel 1892

POETICAL WORKS
Collected Poems (2 Vols) entitled *Poetical Works of George MacDonald* 1893
A Book of Strife in the form of The Diary of an Old Soul 1880

ESSAYS AND LECTURES
A Dish of Orts 1893

SECONDARY SOURCES
George MacDonald — A Bibliography, Joseph Johnson 1906
Recollections of Huntly, George Gray 1892
George MacDonald and his Wife, Greville MacDonald 1924
From a Northern Window, Ranald MacDonald 1911
The Church in the Victorian Era, L. Elliott-Binns 1936
The Letters of Lewis Carroll (2 Vols), edit. Morton N. Cohen 1978
Social History of England, G.M. Trevelyan 1942
A History of Scotland, J.D. Mackie 1964
The Narnia Chronicles, C.S. Lewis 1950-56
Surprised by Joy, C.S. Lewis 1955
George MacDonald: An Anthology C.S. Lewis 1946
They Stand Together, Letters of C.S. Lewis to Arthur Greaves, Edited Walter Hooper 1979

The Hobbit, J.R.R. Tolkien   1937
The Lord of the Rings, J.R.R. Tolkien   1966
The Inklings, Humphrey Carpenter   1978
J.R.R. Tolkein, Humphrey Carpenter   1977
Hawker Country, Joan Rendell   1980
Victorian Wives, Katherine Moore   1974
Fames Twilight, K.N. Colville   1923
Aberdeen University Review, November 1924, article by H.J.C. Grieson
School Library Review, 8December 1964, article by J.M. Hutton
The Golden Key, Professor Robert Lee Wolff   1961

INDEX